SHOPFRONTS

Bill Evans and Andrew Lawson

VNR VAN NOSTRAND REINHOLD COMPANY
NEW YORK CINCINNATI TORONTO LONDON MELBOURNE

Library of Congress Catalog Card Number 81-7626

ISBN 0-442-28253-2

This edition published by arrangement
with Plexus Publishing Limited, London

Printed in Italy

First published in the United States of
America in 1981 by Van Nostrand Reinhold Company
135 West 50th Street, New York, NY10020, USA

Van Nostrand Reinhold Limited
1410 Birchmount Road,
Scarborough, Ontario M1P 2E7, Canada

16 15 14 13 12 11 10 9 8 7 6 5 4 3 2 1

Library of Congress Cataloging in Publication Data

Evans, Bill.
  Shopfronts.

  Bibliography: p.
  1. Stores, Retail — England. 2. Shop fronts —
England. I. Lawson, Andrew. II. Title.
HF5429.6.G7E95   381'.1'0941   81-7626
ISBN 0-442-28253-2   AACR2

Frontispiece: Fribourg and Treyer,
Haymarket, Piccadilly, London

Notes on the Photographs

In this book we have singled out the small independent shops of
England from the vast range of retail outlets that exist. Our intention
has been to record a threatened tradition of English shopkeeping. We
have travelled the country and visited those shops that seem to sum up
one or other aspect of that tradition. We sought out shops that continue
to provide a polite and personal service. We looked for pride and
imagination in the display of merchandise, for skilled craftsmanship in
signs and fittings and for distinctive architecture.

Our choice is personal, idiosyncratic and sometimes irrational. We
went out looking for small shops and came back unable to define them.
A shop should probably be defined as a place where things are bought
and sold. And yet we have included places that trade not in goods but in
services. The cobbler, the barber and the funeral director may not strictly
qualify as shopkeepers, but the High Street, and our book, would be
incomplete without them. By the same token, cafés and restaurants
ought perhaps to have been included, but we have missed them out. And
in case anyone should think us consistent, we have included the eel and
pie house and the temperance bar. In short, we have made our book as a
celebration of people and things that delight us, within the general
scope of shopkeeping.

The photographs have been taken on shop premises; there are no
museum pieces among them. No shopkeeper has asked to be included in
the book. The early photographs of shopfronts (apart from one or two
examples) all belong to owners of existing shops, and we have included
them for purposes of comparison.

Our gratitude is due to the many hundreds of shopkeepers who put
themselves out to allow us to take photographs on their premises. Sadly,
many of them cannot appear in the book for lack of space. A number of
shopkeepers were particularly generous in permitting us to reproduce
early photographs, documents and other historical treasures in their
possession, and we should especially like to thank N. Mann and Sons,
Levy's, England's Dairy, Stroud's, Warwicks, Taylor & Co., Ye Olde
Pork Shoppe, Jesse Smith, F. Cooke, Boscacci, Moresi & Co., A. Hunter
& Son, Lock & Co., and Ernest Napier & Sons. The design for an
Ironmonger & Brazier shopfront from *Architecture of Shopfronts* and the
photograph of Henry Taylor are reproduced by permission of the British
Library; the picture of Campkin & Blackstone is included by permission
of the Cambridgeshire Collection, Cambridgeshire Libraries; and the
picture of Mr John Caton of the Waldorf Hairdressing Salon by
permission of the *Manchester Evening News.*

Finally, our thanks to Martin Parr of Hebden Bridge who advised us
on the many Northern locations and to Michael Williams of Exeter for
help in the South; to our wives Sharon and Briony for their support
with driving and typing; and Colin Webb who brought us together and
suggested that we should collaborate on the book.

Contents

The Kiosk, Lendal, York

Introduction

William Smith, Bradford Road, Bradford, Yorkshire

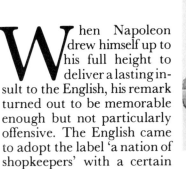

When Napoleon drew himself up to his full height to deliver a lasting insult to the English, his remark turned out to be memorable enough but not particularly offensive. The English came to adopt the label 'a nation of shopkeepers' with a certain amount of pride. The phrase can be taken to suggest qualities of individuality and independence in the national character, although what Napoleon probably meant was that a nation so preoccupied with commerce would be quite unfit for war.

In Napoleon's time there was only one kind of shop and that was the small shop. The man who owned it, ran it, and he usually lived above it too. Today the story is different. The small shops have dwindled in numbers as the retail trade has become progressively dominated by larger shops which carry a broader and sometimes less specialised range of merchandise. The army of small shopkeepers has been retreating from the High Streets where the price war is being won by the big battalions, the multiple chains and the department stores.

But here and there they survive, the small personalised stores, contributing to the character of their streets and inspiring affection and loyalty in their customers. Mr Wigglesworth, Ruby Westlake, Jesse Smith, E. Winpenny, Mr Frank Kirby and Mr F. Pinnington — these ladies and gentlemen or their heirs are still in business and very much at your service. At their emporiums they will be obliged for your custom and the favour of your orders will be greatly esteemed. Here you can buy a hand-made clog or taste a home-cured ham. Here you can have your bread baked to your specification and your groceries delivered in all weathers. Here you can be fitted out with a hat that will be as personal as your own face. Here are shops where the brass on the door is polished every morning; where the baby can be weighed in a basket on the counter; where sterling notes and receipts are sent zooming across the shop by overhead cash railways. Here are butchers that kill their own meat and fishmongers that sell only what they have caught themselves. Their window displays are sometimes very bizarre, sometimes very modest. But look at those articles made on the premises and those that have a strong craft element in their manufacture. You will see arrangements carried out with such care that the display should be treated as an art form in itself. There are items that trigger off memories of childhood; symbols, signs and smells, even products that our grandparents were familiar with in their youth.

In such shops there is a bond of loyalty between shopkeeper and customer. When a shop is put up for sale a value is put on the 'goodwill' of the business. This priceless commodity embraces qualities like service, courtesy and charity. The village grocer is expected to keep the village fed, even if it means extending credit indefinitely to the poorer families. To this day he is sometimes called upon to act as a one-man charity organisation.

Milliner, haberdasher, draper, grocer, ironmonger, corn chandler — the names of some of the trades are evocative of their rich history. Each one has its own peculiar quirks of tradition that distinguish it from the rest. The fishmonger chalks up his prices on a blackboard; the milliner arranges her hats by colour; the ironmonger's display spills out on to the street; the outfitter's shop has a bentwood chair beside the counter; the draper marks the wholesale prices on his materials with a hieroglyphic code. The barber's pole of red and cream stripes, the mortar and pestle of the chemist, the hanging key of the locksmith — these and many more are traditional signs that characterise the trades, and still preserve the gaiety of our High Streets' history.

Travel the country and you may notice subtle distinctions between the shops of the different regions. The most obvious are those connected with regional tastes in foods. The Londoner satisfies his appetite for eels and mash at one or other of the eel and pie houses that are unique to the capital. Up country the taste is for pork, and hence the prevalence of pork butchers in the north. Here and there can be found local styles in sign painting and even regional fashions in shopkeepers' dress — butchers in the north wear a different style of apron from their colleagues in the south. Shops are painted different colours in the regions. In southern market towns most of the shops are mellow and subdued in colour, whereas the industrial towns of Lancashire have gloriously emblazoned shops which compensate for the drabness of their surroundings.

These little distinctions are being erased and the individuality of shops is being reduced as a result of several changes in the nation's shopping habits in the last decade or two. The spread of the chain stores and the self-service system has made it difficult to distinguish one High Street from another. In many ways society benefits from the self-service store: goods are cheaper and more easily accessible to the bulk of the population. Some shoppers even welcome the anonymity of self-service and feel ill at ease under the personal care of a small shopkeeper. But our freedom of choice is jeopardised and the character of our towns is impoverished with every small shop that is destroyed; when mahogany makes way for formica; when mass-produced perspex signs replace the fine old ones, hand-painted and gilded; when engraved plate glass and ceramic tiles are smashed, cabinets and counters removed, and open-plan becomes all the rage.

Census figures show that between 1961 and 1971 the number of small confectioners, tobacconists and newsagents dropped by 37 per cent, grocers and food shops by almost a third, greengrocers and fruiterers by 27 per cent, fishmongers and poulterers by 24 per cent and butchers by 17 per cent. Nearly half the shoe repair shops closed down. In 1973 alone no fewer than 455 pharmacies went out of business.

Possibly the most serious loss to society is the decline of pharmacies. The pharmacist is the most highly trained and specialised of shopkeepers. He can give expert advice to his customers, and thus takes some of the burden off the over-worked family doctor. Only about half the pharmacist's income comes through the National Health for dispensing medicines. For the rest he depends upon the sale of proprietary medicines, toiletries and cosmetics. But the market for these profitable items is being cornered by cut-price drug stores, which can buy the merchandise in bulk, and sell it with untrained personnel. Thrown back on the profits of their dispensaries the pharmacists are finding it increasingly difficult to survive against these unqualified competitors.

Aggressive competition is not the only factor that has forced the closure of small shops. Bureaucracy is another. In recent years every shopkeeper has been shackled with a growing burden of red tape and paperwork. First, the prohibitive selective employment tax (SET) made it difficult for him to employ assistants; now an extra tax burden on the self-employed makes it expensive to employ himself. The transition to decimal currency and the metric system has caused a certain amount of confusion but this is nothing compared with the effects of value added tax (VAT). After a hard day's work behind the counter of his shop, the small shopkeeper has to spend his evenings and weekends going through it all again for the VAT inspector. When the Chancellor alters the VAT level in keeping with his general Budgeting plans, the small shopkeeper is thrown into a flurry of calculations. Many are forced to seek assistance from an accountant, whose services they can ill afford.

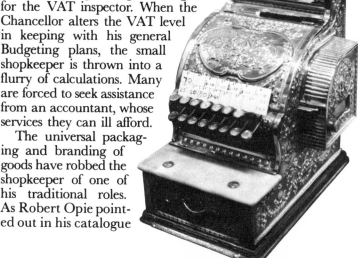

The universal packaging and branding of goods have robbed the shopkeeper of one of his traditional roles. As Robert Opie pointed out in his catalogue

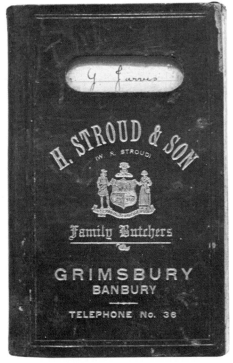

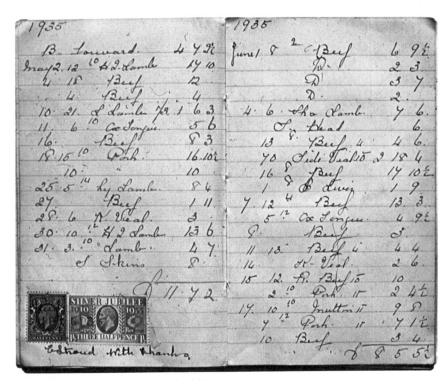

Stroud's, Middleton Road, Banbury, Oxfordshire

A customer's account book for George V 's Jubilee year. Mr Kearse, owner of this butcher's shop, still has no cashier; customers keep their own account books and pay at the end of the week. 'We've never had a wrong'n. We trust them and they trust us.'

to the exhibition at London's Victoria and Albert Museum in 1976, the 'Pack-Age' brought about a revolution in retail trading. Before the days of pre-packed goods the grocer purchased foods in bulk, weighed and wrapped them individually for each customer and set his own price on them. This was a time-consuming process but since he handled personally all the goods that he sold, the grocer could vouch for their quality. Packaging, however, established a direct contact between manufacturer and customer, by-passing to some extent the shopkeeper. Today, the manufacturer labels the package, recommends its price and promotes it by advertising. The customer enters the shop knowing what brand of a particular product he wants, and the shopkeeper's job has become increasingly that of a distributor rather than a salesman. Now he is only qualified to recommend that 'we sell a lot of these'. As shops across the nation continue to carry

identical packaged goods, the regional tastes and distinctions continue to disappear. And as the customers' purchases are increasingly determined by national advertising, the personal service of the shopkeeper might soon be completely dispensable.

The demise of the small personalised shop is not new. As far back as 1836 Charles Dickens, then a young journalist, was lamenting the disappearance of the musty old shops and their replacement by more brash and grandiose establishments. His words, from *Sketches by Boz*, are curiously apt today:
Six or eight years ago the epidemic began to display itself among the linen drapers and haberdashers. The primary symptoms were an inordinate love of plate glass and a passion for gas lights and gilding. The disease gradually progressed and at last attained a fearful height. Quiet, dusty old shops in different parts of the town were pulled down; spacious premises with stuccoed fronts

N. Mann and Sons, Monmouth Street, Covent Garden, London

A family business for five generations, today's trio of picture-frame makers are the great-great-grandsons of the original owner, pictured here in photograph (1) in about 1860. By 1890 their great-grandfather shown here with his family in photo (2) had taken over, and within 20 years in photo (3) his son had joined the business. By 1927, in photo (4), grandfather Mann, on the left, and his son, centre left, were displaying these early photographs, a tradition they continued when they had a new but still open shop front. The present Mann brothers in photo (6) have added the 1948 photograph, (5), to their collection.

4

1

5

2

6

Warwicks, Catherine Street, St Albans, Hertfordshire

Two generations of the Warwick family firm: father photographed during the 1940s (left) and
son taken thirty years later (right). The shop has scarcely changed in between.

*and gold letters were erected instead; floors were covered with Turkey
carpets; roofs supported by massive pillars; doors knocked into
windows, a dozen squares of glass into one, one shopman into a
dozen . . . Suddenly it burst out again among the chemists; the
symptoms were the same, the addition of a strong desire to stick the
Royal Arms over the shop door, and a great rage for mahogany, varnish
and expensive floor cloths. Then the hosiers were infected and began
to pull down their shop-fronts with frantic recklessness . . .*
Dickens was witnessing the early stages of a revolution in
English shopkeeping. Many shopkeepers were becoming
wealthy from trade with the emerging middle classes. The
expansion and amalgamation of their small shops eventually
led to the first department stores. Dickens resented the brash
manifestations of this new prosperity. Little did he realise
that the very shops he abhorred — the gilded and stuccoed
emporia — would themselves appear mellow and sober
beside the developments of a later age of prosperity.

Dickens would have hated the vulgarity of a shop which
must now be counted among the gems that survive — James
Smith & Son, the umbrella warehouse in New Oxford
Street, London. He would not gladly have sat for the
electrically operated hairbrush at Messrs Thomas of St
James's and he would probably have been shocked by the
futuristic interior of Sheila Edwards', the milliner of

Woodford, Essex.

But there are still a few shops that even Dickens would
have adored. He would have enjoyed sitting down to a plate
of eels at Cooke's eel and pie house in Hackney or at Manze's
in Peckham. With their high-backed wooden benches,
marble-topped tables and sawdust-covered floors, these
marvellous institutions, the London eel houses, have a time-
less warmth and friendliness. In Covent Garden Dickens
would be pleased still to find the pet shop where he used to
buy his guinea pigs. Nearby he would be amused to find the
bookshop of Andrew Block, where the books are piled from
counter to ceiling in seeming disarray; in fact, each one is
known intimately to the bookseller and its pedigree is carefully catalogued in his own handwriting.

There are several shops that have passed down from father
to son from Dickens' time to our own. Many a shopkeeper
treasures an old photograph of his shop, with a venerable
ancestor standing before it taken perhaps to commemorate a
special event. Sixty, eighty or a hundred years later the heirs
of these shopkeepers have stood in front of their shops for
their own photographs, with undefeated pride. Sadly our
pictures show some of them on closing day. But others, we
hope, will have sons and grandsons who will stand outside
the same shopfronts and salute posterity in a similar pose.

Jesse Smith, Black Jack Street, Cirencester, Glos.

House Bros, Brewer Street, Soho, London

W. B. Mitchell & Sons, Chapel Street, Penzance, Cornwall

Carter & Son, Minster Street, Salisbury, Wilts.

J. Blundell & Sons, Wardour Street, Soho, London

J. W. Rainbird, Romford Road, Manor Park, London

The Dairy, Camberwell New Road, London

One of the last dairymen in England to deliver his milk by handcart, Mr Owen is up at
5.00 a.m. every day for his two-hour round. This long tradition is shown in one of six scenes
of the Victorian dairyman's work carved on the walls of the dairy opposite.

14

Dairy and Grocer

Dairy, Stroud Green Road, London

The good family grocer scores over his chain-store competitors in four main ways. He offers service, quality, credit, and delivery. He is familiar with his customers' tastes and foibles; he knows where everything is in the shop and he can very often remember the price without looking; if you don't have the correct change the nearest few pennies will do. When it comes to delicacies the small grocer has the edge over the large store. The supermarket has to stock every brand of basic food, and buys in mass; the grocer can choose to sell what he will. He can buy small quantities of exotic foods, or elect to specialise in fine cheese and bacon, and to stock oriental teas, fruit conserves and tins of game soup for the gourmet. He is direct heir to the tradition of 120 years ago, when in Phelp's *The Shopkeepers' Guide* the grocer was recommended to stock fourteen kinds of tea and sixteen varieties of cocoa. Bacon, cheese, dried fruits, tea and coffee, even biscuits are stocked unpackaged so that customers need only buy the weight required. Some grocers still package their own butter and flour and sell them under their own labels.

But the little man in competition with the big stores has his own problems. Buying in smaller quantities he cannot hope to get as advantageous a price as the supermarkets, and it is harder for him to keep his stocks fresh. Sadly the small provisions stores and corner shops are falling increasingly into the role of backstops for the bigger stores. If a customer forgets something at the superstore, he pops into his local corner shop for it. A shop cannot survive long on this casual and irregular trade.

Until a century ago the urban dairyman used to buy cows from country farms when they were in milk after calving. He would keep them in his back yard and look after them until their milk was dried up; this way he could provide fresh milk for his customers. The system was hardly hygienic, as we can gather from Tobias Smollett's description in *Expeditions of Humphrey Clinker* (1775): *But the milk itself should not pass unanalysed, the produce of faded cabbage leaves and sour draff, lowered with hot water, frothed with bruised snails, carried through the streets in open pails, exposed to the foul rinsings discharged from doors and windows, spittle, snot and tobacco quids from foot-passengers, overflowings from mud-carts, spatterings from coach wheels, dirt and trash chucked into it by roguish boys for the joke's sake, the spewings of infants who have slabbered in the tin measure which is thrown back in that condition among the milk for the benefit of the next customer; and finally the vermin that drops from the rags of that nasty drab that vends this precious mixture, under the respectable title of milk-maid.*

Today our pasteurised, sterilised, homogenised milk is piped into the depots from bulk tankers. The massive national dairy firms have a near monopoly of milk deliveries, but here and there small independent firms of dairymen survive, buying milk wholesale from the big creameries but delivering it themselves, sometimes still by handcart.

Of all the shops in the street, the greengrocer has the quickest turnover of stock. Up at dawn every day to select the best fruit and vegetables from the wholesale market, he keeps his display constantly changing throughout the day. Greengrocery is difficult to display because the fruit bruises easily, so often a pyramid is carefully built up, beginning with apples and oranges and topped by garnishes of more delicate produce, such as grapes and tomatoes. Nowadays jet freight and freeze storage allow the greengrocer to stock exotic fruits and vegetables out of season. We can enjoy

England's Dairy, Walmer Road, Notting Hill, London

Mr England's father is seen in the earlier photograph, which dates from around 1920. Most of the enamelled letters of the Bourneville cocoa sign above the door had survived the years, but like Dolly's on page 19, this shop was scheduled for demolition.

Californian strawberries at Christmas time and crisp Australian apples in the spring. And many a greengrocer's window has a cosmopolitan flavour, with yams, paw-paws, green bananas, mangoes, passionfruit and lychees on display. Yet the greengrocer is still something of a High Street almanac, his stock inevitably reflecting the changing seasons in the countryside, even the changing weather. Kent cob nuts, Tunis dates and tangerines in the shops are the cue for Christmas, while summer is announced with new potatoes from the Channel Islands.

One might expect the florist to be a master of window display. But only rarely does his window do justice to his exquisite merchandise, for he must handle his flowers as little as possible if they are to remain fresh for the customer. And there is the danger that if he arranges his flowers too well, his customers might feel loath to break up the arrangement for the sake of their own more modest displays. The florist is the purveyor of symbols. His rose can represent love, gratitude or sorrow to the purchaser. He lives entirely by our desire for celebration, and each celebration calls for its own favourite flowers: snowdrops, lily-of-the-valley at christenings, pink roses for a girl and blue irisis for a boy; freesias and lilies for weddings, chrysanthemums for funerals, red roses for St Valentine's day. We are born, married and mourned to the accompaniment of other men's flowers.

Levy's, Decima Street, Bermondsey, London

The boy in knickerbockers in the 1913 photograph (top) is Mr Levy himself, pictured in the same doorway in 1975 (bottom). The shop has changed very little in the intervening years. In 1975 an elderly lady came into the shop and asked for a tin of Oakey's knife polish, a product discontinued over thirty years ago. Mr Levy stretched up to the top shelf where the polish had stood since the 1930s, wiped the dust off the portrait of Wellington, converted the 9d. price label and charged the woman $4\frac{1}{2}$p.

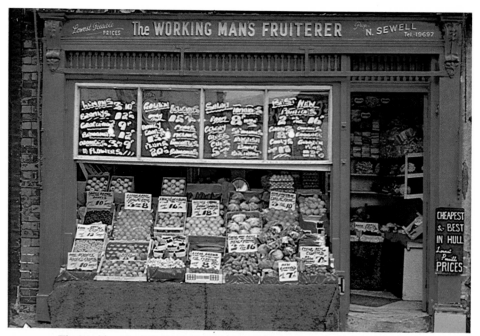

The Working Man's Fruiterer, Beverley Road, Kingston-upon-Hull, Humberside

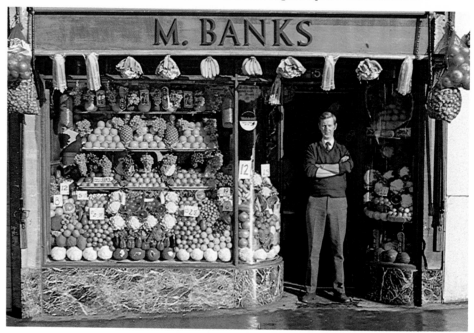

M. Banks, Market Place, Chippenham, Wiltshire

Window displays are a key element in any shopkeeper's trade. Mr Banks's colourful window (bottom) is a magnificent example of what imagination and care can produce. Using only the freshest produce, he puts the hard vegetables at the bottom, and leaves them there for a week. Next come the oranges, apples and pears, which are replaced every couple of days, and finally a layer of soft and delicate fruits and vegetables which, on a sunny day, he changes every two hours or so. Dolly (opposite, top), in London's Ladbroke Grove area, was not as meticulous with

18

Dolly's, Walmer Road, Notting Hill, London

G. Knapp, Market Street, Fowey, Cornwall

her window — or her sales. Never counting the flowers that crammed her shop she would just gather a generous armful into a bunch and put an arbitrary and ridiculously low price on them. Reflected in the window is the scaffolding of the development which was to engulf Dolly's shop shortly after this photograph was taken. Mrs Tregunna, who sells locally-grown flowers and vegetables at Knapps (bottom), gives her window display the appearance of a produce stall at a parish fete.

Hillgay Post Office, Suffolk

The Post Office, Combe, Oxfordshire

The sub-post office is at the centre of community life, a place where the impersonal bureaucracy of the State can be translated into a personal and friendly service. Often doubling as the village store, the sub-post office sometimes still houses the telephone exchange. For economical reasons the Post Office has closed down many such outlets, which are lifelines for pensioners and others drawing State benefits. When the post office closes down it can mean a weekly trek to the next village for the very people least fitted for such journeys.

W. T. Westlake & Son, Fore Street, Hartland, Devon

Ruby Westlake sells just about everything in her tiny village shop. She stocks sweets and stationery, tobacco and cycle spares, petrol and paraffin. Her father, a shoemaker, died in 1949, but she still sells shoes and Wellington boots, some of them with the war time utility mark. The wooden pepper pot contains powder for dusting the feet of potential customers. The large wooden box contains string for wrapping parcels. Her nephew is the village electrician and television repair man.

21

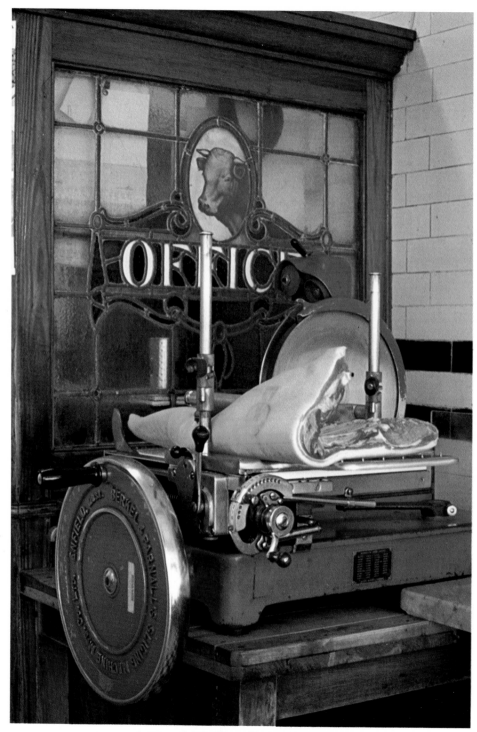

A. Greswell, West Street, Boston, Lincolnshire

Separate offices in many butchers' shops keep the money away from the meat counter. The bacon slicer is a piece of precision engineering indispensable to the pork butcher.

Butcher and Fishmonger

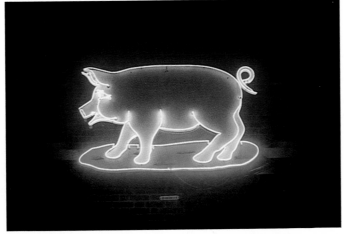

Eli Frusher, East Barnet Road, New Barnet, Hertfordshire

Of all the trades, the butcher and the fishmonger have the most rapidly changing display. Fresh every morning, their merchandise provides a constantly changing parade: each time one piece is taken out, the others are rearranged to fill the space. The butcher puts on a special show at weekends and at Christmas. For the fishmonger Friday is the festive day. At the end of the day's business, the folded tissues over the chrome rail and the parsley in the empty trays are the familiar signs of the trade that indicate the final curtain of the show.

Recent byelaws, brought in to improve hygiene, have taken some of the colour out of the butcher's display. Gone are the days when he could exhibit his prize beef on hooks outside the shop. Photographs taken at the turn of the century record magnificent displays of meat and fowl, but today the hooks grow rusty because the law allows only un-plucked game or meat sealed in polythene to hang outside the shop. Bureaucracy has more in store; a Common Market directive seeks to prevent licensed poultry slaughterhouses from selling Christmas turkeys, freshly killed and plucked and displayed with their entrails in after 1981. But farmer-producers will continue to supply them.

Before the Second World War there were no fewer than 13,000 private slaughterhouses. A high proportion of butchers used to kill their own meat, often doing so in the yards behind their shops. The story of the steer that got away is still told at Jesse Smith's in Cirencester. The steer had been driven into the back yard for slaughter but escaped by running through the busy shop and leaping clean through the window. Now the Common Market regulations are forcing the few remaining small slaughterhouses to close. Soon the sign 'I kill myself twice daily' will be impossible in more

senses than one. However, the policy of large centralised slaughterhouses does bring advantages for some members of the trade. In affluent areas, the butcher sold all the prime cuts, and got left with the offal. In poor districts the cheap cuts went first. But now the butcher can buy parts of a carcass, so that he is not left with cuts that he cannot sell. Nevertheless some of the best butchers still buy their meat 'on the hoof', and some have their own farms. Within living memory a butcher in Bayswater, London, had grazing rights in Hyde Park, and used to drive his sheep through the streets of London to be slaughtered at the back of the shop.

Far removed from the blood and gore of the slaughter-houses are the painted tiles showing cows, sheep and pigs that decorate the façades and interiors of many of the older shops. With benign composure, even complacency on their faces, these animals seem to belong to the world of nursery rhymes and help the customer to forget the bloody aspects of the meat trade. Perhaps the butcher's proverbial cheerful-ness is a protective reaction too, which prevents him from dwelling too much upon his job of handling dead flesh. The 'jolly butcher' is a fair description of most members of the trade. Who ever heard of a morose one? A gang of workers armed to the teeth on one side of the counter and a line of ladies on the other, calls for some sport. In these surround-ings many a natural comedian is born.

Handling meat is a craft trade, and young lads serve an apprenticeship at the block before they are given any responsibility. The beginner starts on the delivery round, and rides the firm's bicycle, fitted with a large wicker basket up front. He has to sweep the sawdust from the floor of the shop and scrub the chopping block, a slab of wood up to a foot thick and deeply bowed in the middle.

To the fishmonger a display of fish is as delicate and as

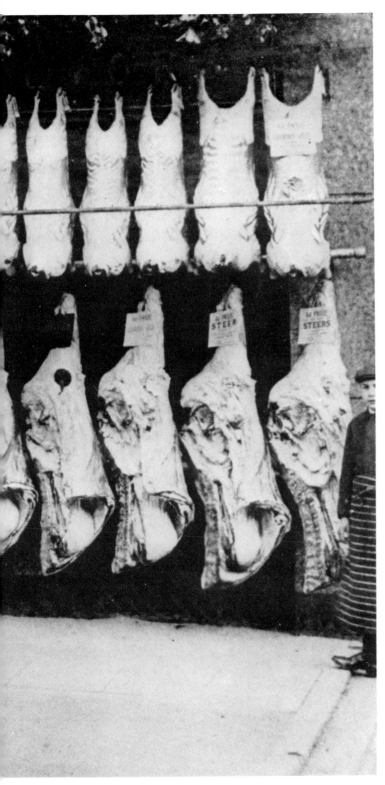

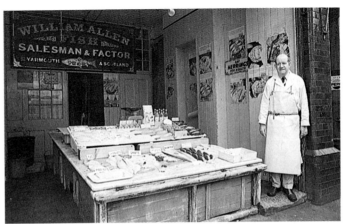

William Allen, Nile Street, Islington, London
Left: Taylor & Co., High Street, Wimborne Minster, Dorset
Christmas is always a time of brisk trade for butchers. This shop, now Wilson's, mounted an impressive display for the holiday season in 1911.

decorative as a spray of flowers and has to be kept as well watered. 'To keep the fish in full bloom the ice must be kept watery' is how one tradesman puts it. One fishmonger in the East End of London regularly saves scales for a local artist, who grinds them into his paints for extra sparkle.

The enterprising fishmonger stocks conger, sea bream, red and grey mullet, as well as the perennial favourites, cod, haddock, plaice and herrings. The tastiest haddock, mackerel and trout are slowly smoked over an oak dust fire in a special shed at the back of the shop. Local tastes vary; in London there is a call for bloaters, whelks and cockles. In the north, hake is a prime fish, and in the far west there is a taste for black seaweed (laver) boiled for nine hours until it becomes a heavy gelatinous mass, and then fried with bacon for breakfast. Weights and measures are varied in the fishmonger's; here kippers are sold by the pair, smelts by the dozen, wet fish by the pound, and shellfish by the pint.

'All the health of the sea is in fish' reads the fishmonger's sign. P. G. Wodehouse's Jeeves is evidence that fish is good for the brain; fish contains on average 18 per cent protein, compared with 12 per cent in eggs and 10-15 per cent in meat.

The fishmonger's shop is usually on the shady side of the street; one fishmonger is proud of the fact that his marble slab has never felt a ray of sunshine. The fish shop is very often open to the street and closed at night by shutters that pull down over the front. In winter, with his shop open to the weather and his hands pink from the constant handling of the fish, the fishmonger is the coldest man in the street. Have you seen a fishmonger cradle his cup of tea in his hands on a cold day? His hands virtually melt around the cup. These discomforts, coupled with the general unpleasantness of cutting off fishes' heads all day, may be a clue to the origin of the fishwife's proverbial coarseness.

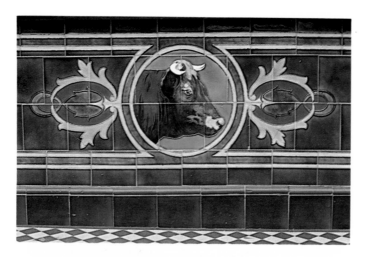

Butcher's Shop, Attleborough, Norfolk

W. R. Mapp, Upper Brook Street, Oswestry, Shropshire

Left: These decorative painted tiles of cows and sheep might help the customer to forget the bloodier aspects of the meat trade. Right: The frontage of this little butcher's shop is very much in harmony with the architecture of the mediaeval building that houses it.

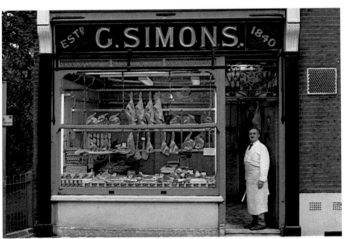

G. Simons, Station Road, Wheathampstead, Hertfordshire

A. J. Cole, Newington Green, Islington, London

F. Wigglesworth, Pendle Street, Nelson, Lancashire

R. Allen & Co., Mount Street, Mayfair, London

Top left: With a slaughterhouse at the back of his shop, Bob Simons can guarantee fresh meat daily. His slaughterman, Roy Downs, is an expert at his trade, one of the few in the business who can carve a 'tapestry' of decorative leaf sprays on the back of a sheep's carcass. Top right: Modesty prevents this team of butchers from stepping over the shopline. Posing for their photograph lays them open to the hoots and comments from their friends on the street. Note that someone has prised off one of the ram's head tiles under the window. Bottom left: This corner shop, like the name of the butcher himself, is typical of a Lancashire mill town. Mr Wigglesworth put on a freshly ironed apron for the benefit of the photograph. Bottom right: Allens have repeated the same window display since the nineteenth century — a row of carcasses of prime English lamb.

Ye Olde Pork Shoppe, Wednesday Market, Beverley, Humberside

This shop used to double as a pub, and the photograph (top) taken in 1945 shows Mr Hillman in front of the Spotted Cow, with a glimpse of his wife arranging the window. In the shop you used to be able to have a glass of ale pulled at the meat counter, and take refreshment whilst your pork was being prepared. Today (bottom) the beer pumps and the Spotted Cow sign have gone but little else has changed.

R. Baker, Prudhoe Street, North Shields, Tyne & Wear

Roy Baker carried on the tradition of his great-grandfather, who introduced smoked saveloys to Newcastle in 1842. The special flavour of the bacon and 'savvies' owed something to the layer of tar, one inch thick, that lined the sides of the smoke hatch. Sadly, Roy Baker's shop was demolished shortly after this photograph was taken and he was stoking the burners not with the usual coal, but with some beautifully carved oak letters that had for many years graced the frontage of his shop.

Jesse Smith, Black Jack Street, Cirencester, Gloucestershire

A classic for its unity of style, this shopfront is a fine example of restrained Art Nouveau design. The distinctive curled lettering, the mosaic floor in the doorway, the contented pig painted on the tiles (top left) all contribute to the effect. Jesse Smith had his own paper bags printed (bottom left) to celebrate the jubilee of George V. The shop's telephone number was changed soon after the bag was printed, but one customer dialled the old number and asked for two shillings' worth of bones. 'We don't sell bones' came the frosty reply. The old number had been taken over by the crematorium.

W. J. Grice, Beeston Road, Sheringham, Norfolk

Bill Grice has always earned his living from the sea. For twenty-seven years a fisherman and a
lifeboatman, he now lands crabs and lobsters off the Norfolk coast. His wife dresses his catch,
and they have established this modest little business between them, Here, crabs and lobsters are
sold by size rather than by weight.

G. Davis, Peckham High Street, London

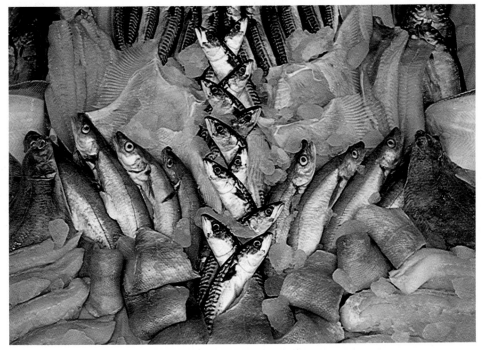

Harry Slater, Cowley Road, Oxford

Two shops that value the display of fish. The owner of Davis's (top) feels he is 'not just selling fish — we're artists. The colours of fish are like flowers in the garden.' For a century the haddock have been smoked in the original shed in the back yard.

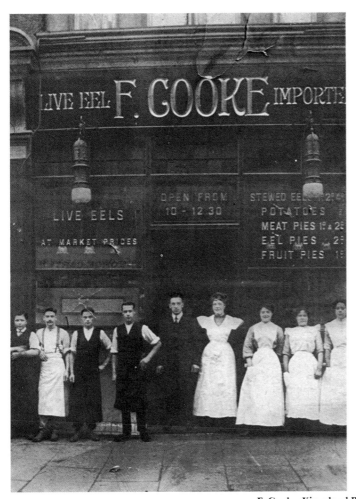

F. Cooke, Kingsland Road, Dalston, London

The eel and pie house used to be a London institution; this shop is now a Mecca for the connoisseur. It was founded in Hackney in 1862 and came to its present premises in 1910 — about the time of the earlier picture. The fourth generation of Cookes is now in command. Two tons of live English eels are kept swimming in oxygenated tanks (opposite) behind the shop, and both restaurant and take-away are thriving.

Baker

The smell of freshly baked bread is the most tempting advertisement in the street. Of all the shopkeepers, the baker who bakes his own bread is the one with the longest queue. He is the first to open in the morning, his windows covered with the foggy mist of condensation and his floor dusted with flour. By mid-afternoon there is usually nothing left on his shelves and he draws the blinds down on an empty shop.

The end of the day's trading marks the start of the next day's baking. The dough has to be prepared so that it can stand overnight to be just right for baking by the morning. The sacred

Dugdale & Adams, Gerrard Street, Soho, London

mixture of flour, water and yeast is pummelled together — sometimes by hand, sometimes by machine — and last thing at night the rubbery dough is laid in wooden troughs to rise. By six in the morning, and sometimes earlier, the baker is back at work, greasing his tins for the first bake. He weighs out the dough, shapes it into loaves and slips them into the oven, using a long wooden paddle to reach right in. Forty minutes later the first loaves are ready to come out, scheduled while still warm for the breakfast tables of his appreciative customers. The bloomer, the cottage loaf, the tin, split tin, sandwich, twist, batch, cob, Vienna, French stick, Coburg, baps and rolls — everyone has his favourite kind of loaf. London is bloomer country; in Newcastle the stottie is the local fancy. They may be made from the same dough but they all seem to taste different.

Before weekends and public holidays the baker has to double, even triple his usual bake, and most bakers have worked around the clock at various times to keep their

customers satisfied. The large bread firms, which deliver their factory-made product to many branches, have a large hold over the market. Being steamed instead of baked, their bread tends to be soggy and tasteless, but it does not dry out and harden as quickly as baked bread, and lasts longer in the shops. Recently there has been a surprising and encouraging trend among the large firms to open up small manufacturing bakeries, producing crispy baked loaves. There are signs that the English are beginning to care about their bread, and that the nation's loaf consumption may be picking up again after having dropped by a third in the last twenty years. This previous fall in bread sales may be linked with the statistic that in 1978, the large white ready-wrapped factory loaf accounted for 51 per cent of consumption compared with 20 per cent for the white unwrapped loaf. With the move back to small bakeries we may yet become a nation of connoisseurs — like the French, who have a bakery in nearly every village and for whom it is a family ritual to collect a loaf or *baguette* from the baker once or even twice a day.

The confectioner paints and sculpts with sweetly-coloured icing sugar. His eclairs and cream slices, his cherry flans and cream buns are works of self-destructive art: to see them is to eat them. His wedding cakes rise white and ornate like miniature mosques; for one imaginative bridegroom a North London confectioner made a cake in the shape of a double bed, complete with marzipan bride and groom between vanilla sheets. The confectioner can write any message chosen in delicious pink calligraphy: a delectable way to mark an occasion.

The Cake Shop, Commercial Street, Halifax, West Yorkshire

Price's Bakery, Quality Square, Ludlow, Shropshire

Mr Price makes about a thousand loaves each day; all are sold from his single shop, or on the
delivery round. One customer has a special loaf baked every other day.

Bill Marder, The Borough, Canterbury, Kent

Temperance Bar & Herbalist, Bank Street, Rawtenstall, Lancashire

Top: Bill Marder, due to retire soon after this photograph was taken, worked a long day. His custom was regular and local — he did not need to put his name above his shop. Bottom: The Temperance movement thrived in the last century when alcohol was cheap and drunkenness rife, particularly in the poorer districts. Temperance Societies forced their members to 'take the vow' of total abstinence from drink. Since Victorian times, Temperance Bars have become a great rarity. This particular shop has its original soda fountain and offers tonics as varied as sarsaparilla and dandelion burdock.

Pam's Pantry, Silver Street, Ottery St Mary, Devon   **Owen's Bakery, The Moor, Falmouth, Cornwall**

Left: It is traditional to bake a wheatsheaf for the harvest festival. The other bread models in this window are an imaginative bit of fun on the part of the baker — and they draw plenty of customers into the shop. Right: The wheatsheaf, symbol of the baker's trade, is beautifully engraved on this shop door.

 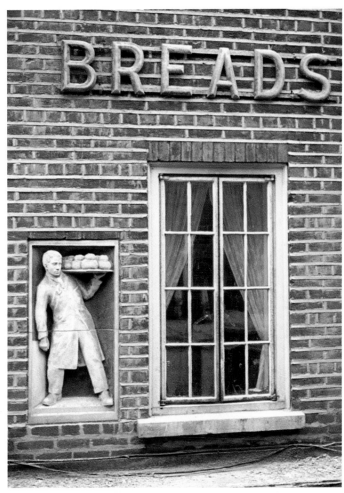

Archer's, Hamilton Road, Longsight, Manchester   **Nordheim's Bakery, Widegate Street, Shoreditch, London**

Left: The cottage loaves are arranged to make a stone wall that fits into the painted land-scape
behind. Right: This spirited and unusual plaque, one of four representing the baker's trade, is
built into the wall, high above street level.

Miller & Co., London Street, Norwich, Norfolk

The carved figure of a Highlander is a traditional emblem of the tobacconist's trade and dates
from the time when many tobacconists were Jacobites.

Tobacconist

H. Simmons, Burlington Arcade, Piccadilly, London

Here is a trade that lends itself to the small personalised business. The sweet and tobacco shop can be run equally well as a profitable hobby or as a full-time business, from a tiny booth in a public entrance way or a full-size shop. The trader in tobacco and sweets depends on the casual custom of the passer-by, and therefore arranges his wares in the most tempting fashion. The tins and packets of tobacco are displayed decoratively behind the counter and the packets of sweets are ranged alluringly in front so that the customer cannot pay for anything without his hand passing over them.

The atmosphere of some of these shops has hardly changed since the time when almost every tobacconist was a Jacobite and displayed a model of a highlander outside the shop, and when a snuff shop could be recognised by the sign of the snuff box above the door. The different blends of snuff are given names as delectable as Masulipatam, Patchouli and Shalimar. Surprisingly, snuff is still very much in demand and is enjoyed by connoisseurs in all walks of life. Snuff is a useful substitute for cigarettes when smoking is not allowed for fear of fire; miners take it underground and pilots flying at night use it to help them keep awake.

Until the late nineteenth century the small retail tobacconist would blend his own tobacco and snuff from the raw materials, which were stored in wooden casks and earthenware pots. Since then blending and packaging of the goods have been taken over by manufacturers who deal with the advertising as well. Before the Second World War there were no fewer than 38,000 different brands available of cigarettes, cigars, pipe tobacco and snuff.

The standardisation of the tobacco trade since then and the reduction in real choice results from the near-monopoly of a few giant firms. This is symbolised by the impersonal shop signs that have been distributed to even the smallest and most intimate of shops. On these standardised signboards the brand name of one or other of these large firms is featured dominantly; the name of the shop owner takes second place.

The pre-packaging of sweets arrived relatively late, and even now it is still not universal. Most people will remember going to the sweet shop as a child, stretching up to hand pocket money over the counter in exchange for a quarter pound of boiled sweets or barley sugars, which the shopkeeper would shake on to the scales from a large glass jar. He would tip the sweets into a white paper bag and then close it with a deft twist of the wrists. Some sweet shops still make some of their own goods. In the summer months, the staff of The Rock Shop in Skegness boil up huge quantities of glucose and, as it cools, knead and stretch it to make lettered rock. Each boil produces about six hundred feet of rock; with ten boiling sessions a day, that means over a mile of rock. Just as glass blowers used to throw left-over glass back into the kiln to make what was called 'end-of-day-glass', so the rock makers throw all the bits and pieces back into the boiling pot to produce aniseed sweets.

The distribution of newspapers from the retailer to the subscribers — still carried out by delivery boys making their rounds on their bikes — involves the same small-scale operations as the sale of tobacco and sweets and the two activities are often amalgamated in one shop. Sometimes country tobacconists or specialist smoker's shops in London also carry rustic walking sticks as a further item of stock. It reflects the small shopkeeper's familiarity with the life and habits of his clientele.

Maisy Trower, Bath Street, Gravesend, Kent

Maisy's shop is about fifty years old and crammed with supplies. The accumulation of goods on
the walls reads like a potted history of the sweet and tobacco trade. Above Maisy's head is a
cartoon of her aunt who used to run the shop, dating from the war days when cigarettes were
kept under the counter and sold only to regular customers.

Skegness Rock Company, Skegness, Lincolnshire

The Rock Shop, Lumley Road, Skegness, Lincolnshire

Bottom: Some Skegness rock being checked for quality. Letters are blocked, moulded and rolled
into the middle of a huge mass of molten glucose which is stretched to enormous lengths.

Ironmonger

The ironmonger is expected to be a walking manual of the home. He is required to have an intimate knowledge of carpentry, plumbing, paints and varnishes, locks, tools and household appliances of every kind. Not only does he supply the goods but he tells his customers how best to use them. As one London ironmonger put it, 'the ironmonger is the Cinderella of the services', meaning that he does the work for all the other trades but receives little thanks for it. He is supposed to carry spare parts for most kinds of domestic appliances although he is not supplied directly by the manufacturers. The wide range of goods that he stocks makes its own demands on the layout of his shop. On yards of shelves and in drawers, boxes and tins of every size he keeps thousands of different articles that only he knows where to find. Within the shop every inch of space is used for display, including the ceiling, which has hooks for hanging brooms and buckets. He solves his display problem by allowing the contents of his shop to spill out into the street. Dustbins, buckets and wheelbarrows are lined up outside the shop.

Hanging street signs in the form of enormously enlarged keys or padlocks signify the locksmith's trade. An earthenware pot, with a lid, set into the wall above the shop is the sign for the oil, colour, paint and varnish store. Builders' and plumbers' shops sometimes make themselves known by placing a lavatory or washbasin incongruously in the window of their shop, or an array of strangely bent tubes, pipes and cylinders.

Decimalisation and metrication are the ironmonger's nightmares, not only because he sells gauges and measures of various kinds, but also because he uses so many different units of measurement himself. He is used to weighing out

Thomas Tingley, Brandon Street, London

nails and tacks by the pound, counting screws and hooks by the gross, selling paints and varnishes by the pint and measuring rope and twine against the brass yardstick set into his counter. All these units are obsolete now, and the ironmonger has had to get used to a new range of measurements. His customary stock-in-trade is changing too. It may not be long before the ironmonger will need to be re-named 'plastic-monger'. Plastic buckets, coal scuttles, water-tanks and so on are universally replacing the traditional galvanised ware, and plastic pipe fittings are used by more and more plumbers in place of copper and lead.

The 'do-it-yourself' shop is heir to the traditional ironmonger in many of our towns. The ironmonger may wrap his nails and screws in a page torn from a telephone directory, but nearly everything in the do-it-yourself shop comes pre-packed. The ironmonger prides himself on service and personal attention, but the very title 'do-it-yourself' seems to imply that the shopkeeper is not always expected to provide advice.

The corn chandler has all but disappeared from our towns and villages, made redundant by today's petrol-powered transport. At the turn of the century the horses' victuallers were almost as common as garages are today. The traditional corn chandler's shop, smelling sweetly of hay and straw, is very rare now and any surviving example is almost certain to be a relic of the last century. Typical features are a solid wooden counter, and large wooden bins to hold the different kinds of corn and meal. The corn is lifted out of the bins with metal scoops and measured by the bushel in cylindrical wooden jugs. The corn store at the back is inevitably patrolled by a battalion of cats. In the market towns the corn chandlers which remain also serve as farmers' seedsmen and

William Flint, Fortess Road, Kentish Town, London

This has been a family business for more than 120 years. The shop is full of relics of the trade, including Kaiser Bill's Firebrick, a gimmick that sold by the thousands during the First World War. Mr Flint says that at one time he was able to provide practically everything people needed for the home; now it is becoming increasingly difficult for him to obtain fittings and spare parts for modern products. 'For every six satisfied customers, I used to turn only one away. Now I'm turning away six to serve one.'

agricultural merchants and in some places the corn and meal merchant is baker as well. In the cities the corn chandlers have expanded their dwindling trade by selling pet foods and bird seed.

There are about 2,000 pet and aquaria shops in England today, catering for most of the domestic needs of our dumb friends. Some shops have their own outfitting departments and pet jewellery counters and are proud to advertise in their windows the latest walking out fashions and jewelled collars. The Englishman's alleged preference for pets before people goes back at least as far as Mary Queen of Scots whose dog was said to be better dressed than her courtiers in a blue velvet suit. How much do the English spend on their pets in a year? Add together the turnover of shops on pet food and equipment, legacies and donations to dogs' homes and other animal charities, boarding fees at kennels, vets' charges, subscriptions and advertising in the thirty-odd pet magazines that are in circulation, fares for pets on trains and buses, entrance fees to pet shows, not to mention the purchase price of hundreds of thousands of pets — and the final figure will be something approaching a staggering seven hundred million pounds.

Vera Haltby, Market Place, Beverley, Humberside

Three hundred years ago this was a tallow chandler's; hooks embedded in the ceiling beams date from then. Candles are no longer made here, but the corn chandling trade is brisk. The massive pair of scales, as old as the shop, is the only hardware present. Hay, straw, and corn make a comfortable environment for four dogs, seven cats — but no mice.

P. Morris & Son, Widemarsh Street, Hereford   **House Bros, Brewer Street, Soho, London**

G. Chapman, Penton Street, Islington, London

Top left: A very fine front, slightly bowed, dating from 1845. The lettering has been fitted well into the arched recesses above the windows. Top right: A superb display of cutlery in a shop that serves Soho's catering trade. Bottom: It takes one hour each morning to arrange this ironmonger's classic display.

Simmonds Stores, Godfrey Street, Chelsea, London

Robert Dyas, Drury Lane, Covent Garden, London

F. W. Collins & Son, Earlham Street, Covent Garden, London

J. Clarke & Sons, High Street, Witney, Oxfordshire

St. Martins Kennels Aviaries & Aquaria, Shelton Street, London

Langs Aquaria, Union Road, Oswaldtwistle, Lancashire

From previous page, top left: A corner shop trading in paint and household wares. The unusual painted jars signify the oil and colour trade. Top right: A drysalter deals in dry powders and oils for household and decorative use. Centre left: This ironmonger's has been run by the same family since 1835. Centre right: Cast iron pillars support this magnificent Victorian shopfront. Bottom left: Established in 1830, this shop included among its customers Charles Dickens, who bought some guinea pigs here. Bottom right: This brightly painted shop is typical of village shops in Lancashire, where strong colours contrast with the sombre surroundings.

Rugham's Pet Stores, Commercial Street, Harrogate, Yorkshire

The latest in terrier wear for a rainy day on the moors.

A. Orridge, Walmer Road, Notting Hill, London

Until it closed in 1974, this was one of the longest established corn chandlers in London. Redevelopment of this site forced Mr Orridge to close his shop but already the steep price of grain on the world market was forcing him to pull out of the business altogether.

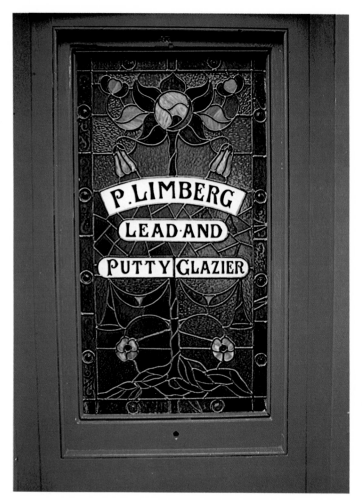

P. Limberg, Columbia Road, Shoreditch, London　　　　　　**The String Shop, Market Place, Stockport, Cheshire**

Left: Builders, decorators and glaziers often work from their homes, and instead of having a shopfront they display the skills of their trade in arresting details on their own houses. Right: A practical and eye-catching display, made with plain balls of string, in an otherwise ordinary window.

Trade Mill, Kingsland Road, Shoreditch, London

The front of this craftsman's workshop displays some intriguing examples of their trade, including signs hand-cut from wood.

Boscacci, Moresi & Co., Whitfield Street, London

This coppersmith's was shortly to close when this photograph was taken in 1975. The workforce had declined to two, from the eleven employed in 1912 when the happy family photograph (top) was taken. Recently the firm repaired pans that were used at Queen Victoria's coronation, thus underlining the permanence of the products of a dying trade.

A. Hunter & Son, Shacklewell Lane, Shacklewell, London

The Hunter family have been wireworkers for two hundred years. The present Mr Hunter's
father is shown (left) at the same shop in 1936.

Fashion Corner, Stockport Road, Levenshulme, Manchester

Decorative black glass panels, a little worse for wear
since the 1930s, still grace the side of this shop.

Ladies' and Gentlemen's Outfitters

Winifred G. Single, Broadway, Bedford

Window displays are important to small, traditional shopkeepers represented within these pages, but they are perhaps most important to those shops selling clothing and its accessories. The butcher, greengrocer, ironmonger and others rely on people's daily needs for the majority of their custom; the outfitter must lure into the shop customers who have no need for (or are not aware that they have) a new dress, suit, or hat. The ladies' or gentlemen's outfitter must therefore use his window as artfully and persuasively as he can.

The gentleman's outfitter is a purveyor of uniforms, of the civilian as well as the military kind. He sells items individually, but he deals in images. Pin stripes and bowlers. Cloth cap and white scarf. Shirts and braces. Jeans and sweater. Frock coat and topper. Spats and cane. The image and its trimmings are inseparable. The gentleman's outfitter must cater for the gentleman's curious whim that his clothes should look as though he has been wearing them for years. Unlike his wife, he feels uncomfortable in anything new. He takes as long to wear in a garment as she takes to wear one out. The extreme conservatism of male dress accounts for some curious relics that survive in the form of official uniforms. Eton boys wear black in mourning for George III. The Navy has only just abandoned the black silk band that was worn in mourning for Nelson. Priests and the boys of Christ's Hospital School cheerfully continue to wear the cassocks that have been their uniforms for centuries. Royal footmen wear the livery and wigs of the eighteenth century. Academics, barristers and judges stubbornly adhere to their impractical garbs. Soldiers, aldermen and freemasons love dressing up. It seems as though anything goes as long as it is old. Ironically the

London Waiting and Loading Regulations ban the wearing of fancy dress within three miles of Charing Cross. If this rule were enforced, most of the London Establishment would be called up before the bench. After the war, and most noticeably in the sixties, the young English gentleman became a bit of a butterfly; perhaps the sartorial glitter of those years was a reaction to the stringencies of wartime uniform. But now we have come full circle and are back to uniforms again, for today's dedicated follower of fashion kits himself out at the army surplus store.

The innovators of men's fashion have been very brave or very rich. James Hethrington was the inventor of the top hat. When he wore it for the first time he was arrested and charged with a breach of the peace, 'having appeared on a public highway wearing a tall structure and having a shiny lustre which was calculated to frighten timid people'. He was fined fifty pounds. Several trend-setting aristocrats have lent their name to garments that they patronised. We have the Wellington boot (originally made for the Duke), the Raglan sleeve and the Cardigan (named after a brace of Earls). The Duke of Windsor, who was earlier the Prince of Wales and then Edward VIII, gets credit for the Prince of Wales check and the Windsor knot for ties. He is also said to have introduced turn-ups on trousers, and to have given royal approval to suede shoes, which had formerly been considered to be in most dubious taste.

Mackintosh and Burberry were men's outfitters whose names have become household words. Charles Mackintosh was a Glasgow merchant who patented a waterproofing substance, made originally from India rubber dissolved in coal tar. Thomas Burberry of Basingstoke invented a system of making yarn waterproof before it was woven into cloth.

The Burberry cloth is weatherproof but porous, so it allows the air to circulate.

Craftsmen who make men's hats have been known as 'gentlemen hatters' since the time of Queen Elizabeth I. A story relates that the Queen was travelling to Tilbury and on the way she was welcomed by a crowd of well-dressed men wearing polished beaver hats. She was struck by their loyalty and smartness and asked who 'those gentlemen were'. On hearing that they were the journeymen hatters of Southwark, she replied, 'then such journeymen must be gentlemen', and the name has stuck.

Like the gentlemen's tailors and hatters, the traditional ladies' outfitters are the very antithesis of self-service. Some of these shops retain the flavour of Edwardian drapery emporia, with service to match: bentwood chairs are ranged along the counter for the customer's convenience as she chooses from the array of merchandise laid before her, and at the end of each transaction any unwanted goods are neatly tucked away in drawers and wardrobes to leave the counter tidy for the next customer. Between the wars the little dress shops, the milliners and the drapers were known as 'Madam' shops. They are brimful of the character of the women and men who run them, and who give them all the love and attention that an elderly member of the family deserves. Their window displays are neatly and impeccably feminine,

each one establishing its independent fashion.

The milliners were originally the vendors of fancy wares from Milan. The early itinerant milliners sold gloves and trimmings as well as ladies' hats, but now the trade is devoted exclusively to hats. Hats are arranged in these shops by colour and not by size or style. The milliner's artistry comes into its own every springtime with weddings and Royal Ascot, and hats and bonnets displayed in the shops around Easter perform their own silent Rite of Spring.

In its long history the corset has played a prominent part in shaping the capricious silhouette of woman. With its supports of whalebone and coiled brass wire it must have squeezed some bodies into permanent disfigurement in the early phase of its career. Tight lacing was strongly opposed by the medical profession and its grave consequences were frequently aired in the *Lancet*. Today the peaches-and-cream colours of girdles and the strangely abbreviated torsos of the mannequins leave much to the imagination.

The drapers were prosperous merchants in the Middle Ages, with their own grandiose Company Hall in the City of London. In the nineteenth century they flourished and some of the more successful ones expanded to become the first department stores. Some of the ladies and gentlemen working today in the small drapers' shops served their apprenticeship in the haberdashery department (or 'habby' for

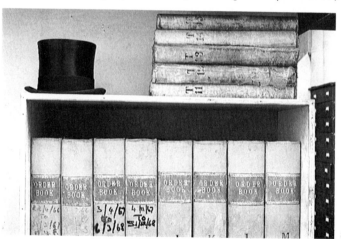

Lock & Co., St James's Street, St James's, London

Anscombe's Drapery Emporium, Leyton Road, Harpenden, Hertfordshire

Left: Lock's account books show records of dealings with Londoners of distinction since 1676.
Right: This shop boasts probably the largest cash railway system in Britain.

short) of a big store, a job that would test the patience of a saint, sometimes spending an hour with a customer to choose just the right ribbons and a matching thread, and all for a few coppers. Still, working conditions for assistants in the twentieth century would have sounded luxurious to their Victorian counterparts. Drapers' shop assistants usually lived in, and working hours were incredibly long. One testimonial to this is the story of an assistant who served for four years and never once had the opportunity to put on his hat and coat except on Sundays. It took an act of Parliament to ensure that female shop assistants should be provided with chairs on which to rest while not serving.

The traditional laundry and bagwash is a service that may soon disappear altogether. Launderettes and domestic washing machines should see to that. But despite these convenient winds of change there still survive the occasional firms that act as valets and take in your dirty washing, clean, press and starch it, and parcel it up in that particular blue wrapping paper that fades with the light. Even the legendary Chinese laundries steam away in forgotten corners.

The small shoe merchant must rely almost exclusively on his windows to display his goods, for the space inside his shop is filled from floor to ceiling with columns of labelled boxes. One shopkeeper estimated that for each style of shoe it is necessary to stock no less than seventy pairs, each one a different combination of size, fitting and colour. A shoe shop with a choice of, say, one hundred styles, may therefore have in stock seven thousand pairs of shoes.

Shoemaking became mechanised around the middle of the nineteenth century. Before that time every village would have had its own shoemaker, fashioning footwear by hand for the whole community. Shoemaking has been known as 'the gentle craft', perhaps by virtue of its patron saint, Crispin, who is said to have supported himself by making shoes while preaching as a missionary. The gentle craft survives still, drawing its patronage from the rich, who can still afford the luxury of bespoke shoes, and crippled people, for whom the individually shaped shoe is necessary. Many people wear comfortable, healthy, wooden-soled shoes without realising that the clog is an indigenous English shoe, and as much a part of the north country as black pudding and cotton mills. But clogmakers, or 'cloggies' as they are known, have become few and far between in Lancashire, Yorkshire and Cumbria. Those that remain are enjoying a growing demand for clogs for factory and farm wear, and for social and medical use too. With soles carved by hand to fit the customer's feet, uppers of red, brown or black leather, and hand-made brass tacks to hold them all together, the English clog is as comfortable and as distinctive as many a more fashionable shoe and much cheaper.

Drapers Shop Window, Leamington Spa, circa 1909

The Net Centre, Charlotte Street, Fitzrovia, London

Left: A contemporary celebration in lace. Right: This shop proclaims its trade with a fan dance
of lace and net as a window display.

E. Winpenny, High Street, Stockton-on-Tees, Cleveland

P. Phillips, Pembridge Road, Notting Hill, London

Silver's, Broad Street, Worcester

Floré Cooper, St Benedicts, Norwich, Norfolk

Top left: Though men's fashions and the method of displaying them have changed, little else has altered on this inviting Edwardian shopfront. Top right: Now closed, this small and unpretentious shop had been selling second-hand riding boots and military clothes for years before such gear became fashionable. Bottom left: A good example of a 1930s shopfront in which the display area has been increased by a free-standing show cabinet in the middle. Bottom right: Hats are arranged by colour and not by style.

Issie Lipman, Beverley Road, Kingston-upon-Hull, Humberside

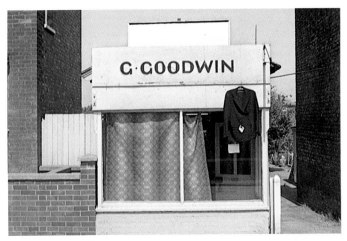

G. Goodwin, Sutton Bridge, Lincoln

Western's Laundry, Turnpike Lane, Wood Green, London

Fung Kee Laundry, Holgate Road, York

Top left: A handwritten sign inside Issie Lipman's shop sums up his philosophy of life: 'God grant me the serenity to accept the things I cannot change, courage to change the things I can, and wisdom always to tell the difference.' Top right: The proprietor of this small shop thought the weather was too hot for a window display that day. 'Anyway,' he said, 'the coat says I'm open.' Bottom left: The sunrise motif is a common symbol for the laundry trade. Bottom right: A Chinese hand laundry, the butt of many an old joke, but here a relative newcomer in one of England's oldest cities.

F. Pinnington, Burnley Road, Todmorden, West Yorkshire

Mr Pinnington is one of just a handful of cloggies still working in Britain today.

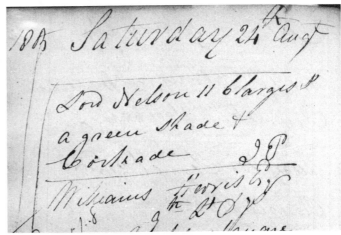

W. S. Hirsch, North Bar Place, Banbury, Oxfordshire

Lock & Co., St James's Street, St James's, London

Left: A London tailor who moved to the country. The expression 'sparing the boot' comes from the tailors' cross-legged position shown here: when one tailor wanted to borrow money from another, he would ask him to spare the boot; the lender would then chalk up the loan on the sole of his boot. Right (top and bottom): A shop that has supplied hats for history. Nelson came to Lock's before the Battle of Trafalgar to be fitted with the cocked hat with a special eye shade. He was wearing this when mortally wounded. His purchase is recorded in the firm's order books (page 60). Another of Lock's customers, a Norfolk squire named William Coke, wanted strong hats for his gamekeepers. Between them, Lock's and Mr Coke designed a hat and commissioned a certain William Bowler to make it up for them. It came to be known as the 'bowler' (or 'derby' in America), but Lock's still call it the 'coke' after the gentleman who bespoke it.

Sheila, Woodford Parade, Woodford, Essex

This superb example of shop architecture is as fresh today as when it was built in 1932. Sheila Edwards and her husband consulted a well-known designer on what would be best for the manufacture, display and fitting of hats. The etched glass doors (opposite; top left) illustrate bird's eye views of hats. Every detail inside and outside the shop down to the metal blinds (top right) and the waste bins is in the best tradition of Art Deco. Sheila, who is in her seventies, thinks nothing of working eighteen hours a day making hats. 'It's the only time I'm really happy. I just can't sit still.' Her dedication to her work is reflected in the general atmosphere of the shop, where every hat is an individual creation — a small work of art which celebrates the joy of craftsmanship and design. Sheila is a credit to the milliner's trade.

Brent & Sons (Army and Navy Stores), Station Road, Fowey, Cornwall

Mr Brent has been catering for servicemen stationed in Cornwall for more than fifty years. His
shop has no connection with the more famous store of the same name.

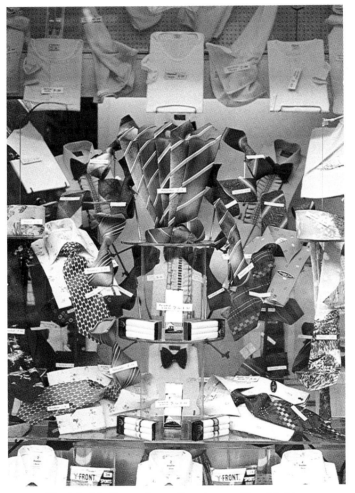

M. Yanovsky, Whitechapel Road, Whitechapel, London

Hazel Smith, Regent Street, Leamington, Warwickshire

Chel Crowe, Wentworth Street, Spitalfields, London

Left: Care, patience and attention to the smallest detail make this an impeccable display of shirts and ties. Top right: Mrs Sinclair is the grand-daughter of the original Mr and Mrs Yanovsky, and she is proud to carry on in the family tradition of corsetiers. 'My grandmother called them La Gaine, my mother called them corsets or stays, and we call them a foundation.' Bottom right: The Crowe family trade as children's outfitters in their shop in Petticoat Lane, centre of London's Jewish community. The animated mannequins were modelled on Shirley Temple, child idol of the 1930s.

Hairdresser and Chemist

The hairdresser's shop has been through as many changes as the hairstyles that have evolved within it, and we illustrate only a few types of shop from the wide range that exist. What do they have in common, the grandiose gentlemen's establishment and the unisex parlour? The archetypal army barber with his pudding basin and the suburban ladies' salon with frilled lace curtains that would not look out of place in a poodle parlour? The trimmings are different but the essence of the business is the same — a craftsman moulding the appearance of his customers and fashioning a style to satisfy their private whims and fancies.

Ivans, Jermyn Street, St James's, London

A part of the history of the trade is condensed in the cream and crimson stripes of the traditional barber's pole. The stripes represent blood and bandages and the symbol dates from the days when the barber was surgeon too. He would apply leeches to let blood, and he would draw teeth as well as cutting and dressing the hair. A legend of this phase in the hairdressers' history is Sweeney Todd, the demon barber of Fleet Street, who was alleged to have been a little liberal with the blood letting, and who is celebrated in Victorian melodrama and song.

The Victorian and Edwardian eras produced palatial gentlemen's saloons with marble sinks, beaten copper basins, carved mahogany fittings and the electric hairbrush. The 1920s and '30s were a golden age for the trade, when the public began to ape the hairstyles of their favourite 'moving picture' stars. Etched glass doors, neon signs and a range of streamlined busts of the period are still the focal points of many shops. Twenty years later it was Elvis Presley and Tony Curtis who set the fashion in hairstyles for the impressionable teenagers of the day, and Denis Compton who

promoted the favourite dressing for the hair. The styles were almost universally accepted and as hairdressers became 'stylists to the stars' the old name of 'barber' became unfashionable.

Inside the barber's shop there is generally a feeling of congeniality. Many good jokes and stories are born and distributed here. Before betting shops were made legal the barber would often take bets and a copy of *The Sporting Life* was usually close at hand. Today the barber is still an expert on the turf as well as the purveyor of local news. In the rather adult club-like atmosphere many boys awaiting their turn have been introduced to the finer points of the opposite sex through overheard conversations and naughty photographs, discreetly tucked away and just as discreetly passed around.

No other shopkeeper has such a stringent apprenticeship as the chemist. He has to spend three years at college, followed by a year in practice before he can qualify as a pharmacist, a preparer and dispenser of drugs. He must display his certificate of registration in his shop, and throughout his career he is answerable to the Pharmaceutical Society of Great Britain in all his professional conduct. With all that education behind him the chemist would like to be able to apply his knowledge to the full. But his skilled tasks of mixing and dispensing medicines are being taken over by the pharmaceutical companies, who produce more and more drugs in standard packages.

The origin of the chemist's trade is shrouded in the queer history of the occult. Alchemists and astrologers, quack doctors, herbalists and witches are the ancestors of this now highly scientific profession. The three witches in *Macbeth* were not so far removed from the reality of Shakespeare's time. Lists of seventeenth century drugs include such treat-

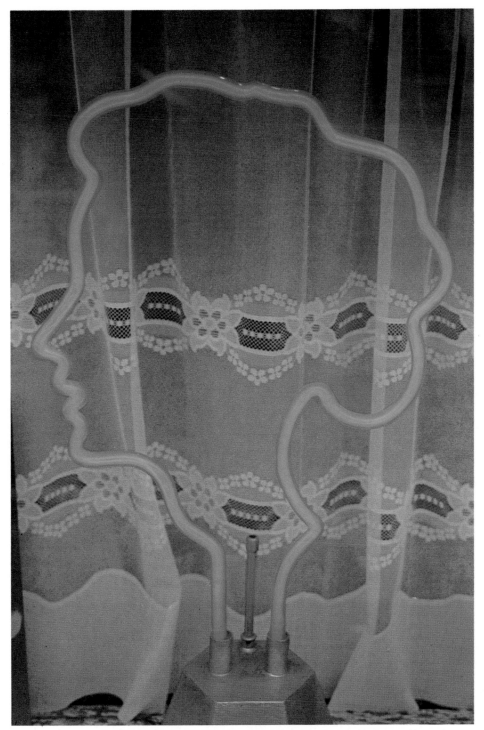

Clarkes Continental Styling, St Paul's Road, Islington, London
The hairstyle dates this good neon silhouette of the 1940s.

71

William McEwan, Craven Road, Paddington, London

Mr McEwan ran this shop single-handed until he retired and the shop closed early in 1975. 'I'm just an old-fashioned chemist. People come in and ask if I sell nylon tights and I say no. I didn't sit up till three in the morning studying just to sell tights. I spent two years at College and then I was an apprentice for four years at 2s. 6d. a week. That's six years training — longer than a doctor's.'

ments as powdered toads for dropsy and nose bleeds; human skin worn below the knees to cure cramp; peacocks' excreta for epilepsy and vertigo; millipedes taken whole to cure jaundice and asthma; the seahorse as an antidote to the bite of a mad dog.

The chemist's sign is still the mortar and pestle which were used by the apothecaries to grind up their herbs and spices. The apothecaries themselves were offshoots of the grocers, originally the dispensers of herbs. From the seventeenth century to this day, herbs for drugs have been grown in the Chelsea Physick Garden in London. Cinchona, aloes, hyoscyamus niger, coriander – the euphonious names of some of the traditional apothecaries' products can still be read in the gold lettering on many a chemist's mahogany drawer.

With half the population suffering from bad vision, the optician's services are much in demand. He may not legally practise before he has passed his examinations after four years of study. His most important role is the selection and adjustment of lenses, but his fashion-conscious clientele demand that their spectacles should be elegant as well as functional. The classic optician's sign of an isolated pair of bespectacled eyes was a dominant image in F. Scott Fitzgerald's *The Great Gatsby* and is still a standard fixture above some optician's shops. One enterprising firm has gone a stage further with shopfronts themselves designed to look like spectacles, so that the windows become the eyes and the door the nose.

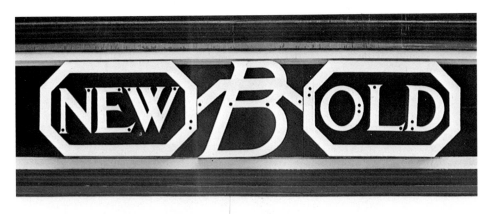

Newbold Optician, Piccadilly, Hanley, Staffordshire

Clement Clarke, Cheriton Place, Folkestone, Kent
Two arresting shop designs which make appropriate use of the spectacle motif.

Gentlemen's Hairdresser, Parade Square, Lostwithiel, Cornwall

By no means inevitable, a barber with a good head of hair. The colours of the barber's pole have been picked out in the paintwork of the shop, although the particular red is a distinctively Cornish choice. The blackboard tells the times of opening.

Syd's, White's Row, Spitalfields, London

G. F. Trumper, Curzon Street, Mayfair, London

Gentlemen's Hairdresser, Friar Street, Worcester

Top left: This barber's shop is a spic and span unit found in London's East End. Syd draws his trade mainly from nearby Spitalfields market. Bottom left: A long-established firm with many famous names amongst its clientele. The front, with its rich lettering, its Royal credentials and lavish display, gives promise of meticulous attentions within. Right: This barber has been cutting hair in this shop since 1919. 'All the toffs used to come to me. If I had a book of all the people I'd done it would stretch from here to Brummejum (Birmingham).' Neither decimalisation nor inflation has gone to his head: he still charges four shillings.

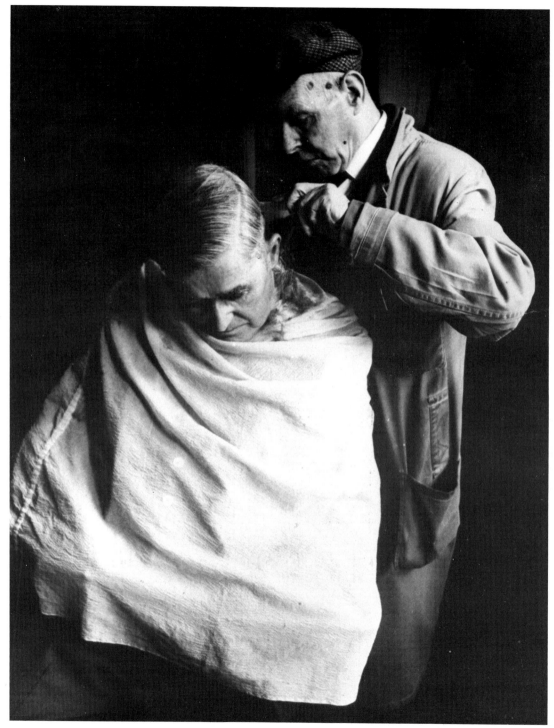

Gentlemen's Hairdresser, Friar Street, Worcester

Inside, the shop is the parlour of a private home. Customers keep their caps on too until their
turn comes to sit in the barber's chair.

The Waldorf Hairdressing Salon, Clarence Street, Albert Square, Manchester

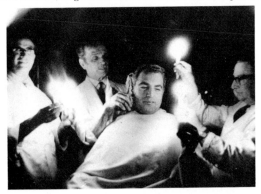

Top: John Caton is the proprietor of this magnificent Edwardian hairdressing saloon, where nothing much has changed since 1908. It features bevelled mirrors, marble and copper sinks, and seats raised by hand jacks. Waiting seats have wide arm rests for those wishing a manicure, and the shop still has an infra-red booth in the back room and a wart-removing machine. Bottom: Undeterred by the electricity black-out in 1972, Mr Caton and his staff cut hair by candlelight.

O. Vellucci, The Quadrant, Green Lanes, Winchmore Hill, London   **Ladies Hairdresser, Freeman Street, Grimsby, Humberside**

Left: An Art Deco portrait, etched on a glass panelled door. Right: These models were
reproduced by the thousands for window displays and reception areas.

Frank Heap, Church Street, Haslingden, Lancashire

Meacher, Higgins & Thomas, Crawford Street, Marylebone, London

Bannister, High Street, Tewkesbury, Gloucestershire

Top left: The plants in the window are more appropriate symbols of this trade than all the familiar cosmetic advertisements. Bottom left: Thomas Meacher, the first partner in the firm, was established as a chemist in 1814. Prescription books of the 1890s record the dispensing of best speckled leeches at four shillings a dozen. A proprietary compound called Yanatas (You are now able to avoid seasickness) had a testimony from the Tzarina of Russia. Right: The shop is Victorian, but it makes good use of the early seventeenth-century building.

D. Durbin, Walworth, London

Cut'n'Blow, Churwell, Yorks.

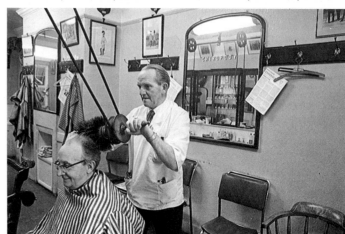

Thomas, Duke Street, St James's, London

Mr & Mrs Thomas Hamnet, Coten End, Warwick

Left: Thomas Hamnet was born over this barber shop, which is housed in a fifteenth-century building. He came into the trade as a lather boy when only seven years old. His sister used to do the shaving; now his wife Mabel helps out. Tom talks about all the smiling faces he remembers on his bench: 'Now they're all gone, and everybody sits there with faces like spare dinners.' Top centre: A gas-heated chrome towel steamer. Top right: An enterprising housewife's home industry. Bottom right: This motorised hairbrush is connected by a rubber belt to a wheel on a shaft that runs the whole length of the shop, with a fitting for each chair. The shop provides copies of the Eton College Chronicle for reading matter and its walls are adorned with sporting prints and hunting trophies.

Platt's, Stockport Rd., Manchester   **J. R. Brown, Beverley, Humberside**

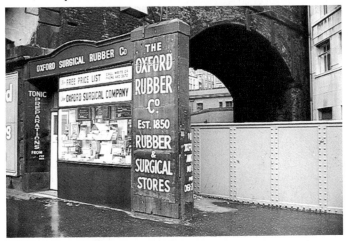

The Oxford Surgical Rubber Co., Oxford Street, Manchester   **Wilson & Dickinson, George Street, Bath, Avon**

Top left: This neon sign is fifty years old. Top centre: This doorway was once the entrance of a chemist's shop. The serpent in Greek mythology was a symbol of healing, and the pole represented power from the wand of Hermes. Bottom left: This shop is built at a daring angle on the pavement and is totally dwarfed by the bridge and a giant Refuge Insurance building behind it. Right: Founded in 1823, this shop's present front was put up in 1898. Its magnificent door, complete with flamboyant Art Nouveau tracery, was made especially wide so that the invalid gentry, visiting Bath to take the waters, could get into the shop in their Bath chairs.

The Specialist

Under the banner of the specialists come those shops that engage in a great variety of skilled activities. The sports shop, the pawnbroker, the photographer and the tattooist, the saddler and the umbrella shop — here are many of the personalities who bring colour to the English street; an assorted group of individualists whose services we require infrequently but who remain essential to the community.

There are shops that make other men's hobbies their profession. A whole nation of shopkeepers exists to serve the other nation of football and cricket fanatics, pigeon fanciers, stamp collectors, darts players and crossword puzzle fans. Every hobby and pastime supports an industry of professionals behind it. There are men who spend their time twisting sheep's intestines to make gut for tennis racquets; others who breed bluebottle maggots (ironically called 'gentles' in the trade) to supply bait for the three million men and their dogs who go fishing every week.

By the same logic that a cudgel for killing fish is called a 'priest', the pawnbroker was known as the 'uncle' in the streets over which he held sway at the time of the Depression. He enabled families to hover just above starvation level by buying their belongings from them at the beginning of the week and trading them back at a profit at the end. On a Monday morning there would be a queue of women outside the shop, each with her husband's best suit to pawn; at the end of the week she would be back to redeem it. The husband would blithely wear the suit on a Sunday without knowing about the transactions that went on.

Unwilling to pawn their best clothes and jewellery if they could help it, some customers tried to trick the local broker by substituting dubious goods in the familiar brown paper

James Smith & Sons, New Oxford Street, London

parcels. One pawnbroker in Manchester was given a typical package and told that it was a suit and hat. Soon his shop began to smell. The locals were jubilant. After a frenetic search he found the offending parcel. It contained a pig's head, by then unbelievably putrid. He became known as Piggy Riley, which remained his name to his dying day. The name still lives on in the Ancoats district of the city.

The pawnbroker's hold over people's lives has almost completely disappeared and the pawnbroker's shop itself has become scarce. Many have converted to straight jewellery and silverware businesses. The design of the jeweller's shop is governed by the nature of his wares. The objects that he sells are small and need to be displayed close to the glass of the window; more goods can be included by increasing the surface area of the window. The simplest way is to build a bow front, for a rounded window has a greater surface area than a flat one crossing the same space. A more elaborate version of this device is a shopfront with a door set well back from the street; the windows curve round to meet the door, making an alleyway of glass through which the customer has to pass before entering the shop.

Paradoxically antique shops are relatively new arrivals. They often occupy old and lovely premises, but this is deceptive since they are rarely long-established businesses themselves. Antique dealers conserve their shops with loving care, but there remains a feeling that it is possible to conserve something *too* well — by smoothing down the rough edges one risks extinguishing the lively character that is a keynote of the traditional English shop.

Still, in some dusty forgotten street, one comes upon the real thing, a shop that has no pretensions to sell anything other than junk. In *Sketches by Boz* Charles Dickens described

Sheppards Market, Church Street, Stoke Newington, London
Mr Sheppard (the shorter one) and his assistant make an interesting duo among their goods —
it's difficult to imagine them trading in anything else.

the assorted wares to be found in one such shop:

Our readers must often have observed in some by-street, in a poor neighbourhood, a small dirty shop exposing for sale the most extraordinary and confused jumble of old, worn-out, wretched articles, that can be well imagined. Our wonder at their ever having been bought, is only to be equalled by our astonishment at the idea of their ever being sold again. On a board, at the side of the door, are placed about twenty books — all odd volumes, and as many wine-glasses — all different patterns; several locks, an old earthenware pan, full of rusty keys; two or three gaudy chimney-ornaments — cracked of course; the remains of a lustre, without any drops, a round frame like a capital O, which has once held a mirror; a flute, complete with the exception of the middle joint; a pair of curling-irons, and a tinder-box. In front of the shop-window, are arranged some half-dozen high-backed chairs, with spinal complaints and wasted legs; a corner cupboard, two or three very dark mahogany tables with flaps like mathematical problems; some pickle-jars, some surgeons' ditto, with gilt labels and without stoppers; and an unframed portrait of some lady who flourished about the beginning of the thirteenth century, by an artist who never flourished at all; an incalculable host of etceteras of every description. . .

Rarely does one come upon a second-hand bookshop with the same atmosphere of eclectic chaos. The best of the antiquarian bookshops have the ambience of a private library, slightly decayed perhaps but giving only an impression of wonderful disarray. The customer has the illusion that he might find an unrecognised treasure on the next shelf. But the bookseller has an uncanny knowledge of his stock, and follows trade journals and sale catalogues to keep up with the prevailing prices.

In its early days, photography was taken up largely by portrait artists as a profession and by rich and eccentric

Harlip, Bond Street, Mayfair, London
Society portraiture at its best, Mme Harlip's pictures have that romantic softness characteristic
of 1920s photography. With rents and rates trebled in recent years she even finds it hard to cover
her expenses. But she works for the love of it: 'It is my life; if I didn't work I would die.'

amateurs as a hobby. A century ago the photographer was
regarded rather like a magician, fixing the image of his sitters
with mysterious chemical reactions and stealing some of
their soul in the process. Something of the conjuror survives
in the professional photographer of today, who hides like
Mephistopheles under a huge black cape and commands the
severe attention of serried ranks of schoolchildren. 'Cheese' is
the magic word of the photographer; less colourful than
'abracadabra' but better calculated to relax the muscles of
the face. At the church door the professional photographer
takes over as master of the wedding ceremony, arranging the
participants in relaxed attitudes that usually contradict their
true experiences of the event.

The studio photographer still provides the service that
used to be the prerogative of the portrait painter or minia-
turist — to provide an idealised picture of the sitter, with all
warts removed. The camera can be made to tell a beautiful
lie under the gentle lights of the studio and through the soft-
focus eye of the portrait lens. The photographer's shop
window is a gallery of portraits, with prime examples of his
craft often printed on simulated canvas and displayed on
easels, giving the impression of hand-made paintings in oils.
As in painting, a good photographic portrait says as much
about the personality of the artist as of the sitter. The best
photographs are those that seem to have been hand-drawn
with light.

In the same tradition of craftsman-shopkeeper, but with
far more primitive origins, is the tattooist, who exists for the
same purpose, to beautify his customers in their own eyes.
Predictably the tattoo shop is found near docks and bar-

Dennis Noble, Camberwell Church Street, Camberwell, London

A non-society photographer, Dennis Noble is such a well-known personality in the area that he hardly needs to advertise.

racks, but one maverick can be found operating under the disapproving eyes of the housewives of Bath. The tattoo shop has a macabre atmosphere, compound of the surgeon's clinic and the occult imagery of fiery dragons, eagles and mermaids, and the popular graphics of love. The tattooist's work is seasonal, reaching a peak in high summer when his art receives its maximum exposure to the light of day. Seasonal too are the favoured images of tattoos. In spring the rose blooms on many a tattooed arm. In summer there is a demand for aggressive designs, such as black panthers, eagles and the like. In autumn, swallows fly briefly into vogue. One tattooist, working near an army barracks tells of the long queues whenever there is a fresh call-up for Ulster. 'That's the thing about our business; as long as you've got love and war you'll always have tattooing.' Tattoos are almost un-

removable and so there is scope for some dreadful regrets; many a forgotten sweetheart is embalmed by name for ever on her lover's skin if not his heart. One tattooist tells the story of the time he accidentally wrote 'Mice' on a young girl's hand, instead of 'Mike'. Luckily he managed to adapt the word before the customer noticed. It is not surprising that a tattooist at Kings Cross in London felt the need to emblazon his 'Tattooist's Prayer' in oriental script above his door.

The saddler is a craftsman shopkeeper of the traditional kind, making most of what he sells and very often living above his shop. Curiously his craft is enjoying a boom after a desperate struggle for survival at the turn of the century when horse transport gave way to motorised vehicles. The saddler has had to adapt his trade, and can turn his hand to anything in leather — belts, bags, dog collars and muzzles,

Bart. J. Snowball, Dean Street, Newcastle-upon-Tyne   **Janson's, Great Russell Street, Bloomsbury, London**

Left: Tom Stevinson has been a saddler for sixty years. His family has been making saddles since 1786. Right: Mr Janson receives butterflies from all over the world, and prepares them for collectors, as did his father and grandfather before him.

fittings for sheep and cattle as well as conventional horse saddles and harnesses.

The umbrella is a commodity that never seems to go out of fashion, although it is no longer the all-weather necessity it was in Victorian times, when ladies strove to protect their lily-white complexions from the sun. Interestingly the first umbrellas were held upside down because nobody had invented a clasp to keep them from opening out when they were held the other way. In the nineteenth century gentlemen would often have swordblades built into the handles of their umbrellas to keep the street brigands at bay. Today when it rains, customers scurry into the umbrella shop to buy their portable protection. Much business is done for the very reason that they are so portable — and therefore lost with

W. J. Breedon & Co., High Road, Leyton, London　　　　**Joe's Shoe Repairs, Toynbee Street, Whitechapel, London**

Left: Bob Breedon's family has been making cricket bats since 1833. His shop is well-placed beside the Essex ground, but business has declined so much that he is forced to earn a living as a newsagent. Right: Joe took over this shop twenty-eight years ago even though the property had been condemned since 1934. He only moved in as a temporary measure for six months and now, though the ceiling has collapsed on him, he carries on regardless.

greater frequency than any other clothing accessory.

Cobblers tend to be all-round leather craftsmen too and will mend handbags and briefcases as well as skilfully repairing shoes. Working in his shop window, with a row of tacks gripped between his lips, the cobbler taps away at an amazing speed between attending to his customers. He then chalks the name on the sole of the shoe, passes the time of day, and goes back to his bench for a little more tack-tapping before the next interruption. This craftsman shopkeeper has become a rarity; between 1961 and 1971, fifty per cent of the shoe repair shops in this country closed down. In part this is due to the decline of recruits to all kinds of craft trades but it also stems from the built-in obsolescence of the mass-produced fashion shoe.

87

A. H. Nightingale, Oscar Road, Broadstairs, Kent

Fred Tout, High Street, Dulverton, Somerset

The Dart Shop, Forest Road, Walthamstow, London

Frank Kirby, St Benedicts, Norwich, Norfolk

Top left: Behind the jumble of stamps in the window (inexpensive ones, since the sun will bleach them) lies an office that could be mistaken for a lawyer's consulting room. Top right: It is the wise angler that consults the local fishing shop before setting out along unfamiliar water. The Exmoor trout and salmon are distinctly partial to this local fly dresser's concoctions. Bottom left: A set of darts, made to measure, precision-turned in bronze and expertly balanced, can be purchased here for the price of an off-the-peg suit. Bottom right: The third generation of his family in the cycle business, Frank Kirby says that all the wheels that now come in from the factory have to be made true.

L. Cornelissen & Sons, Great Queen Street, Covent Garden, London

An artists' and restorers' shop, artistically restored. All too often when a shop changes hands the new owner cannot wait to rip it all apart. But at Cornelissen's the new proprietor has cherished the original features of the shop and lovingly restored them. The gold seals in the window record prizes for artists' colours in Paris in 1867 and 1878 and in Vienna in 1873. The shop still sells pigments in powdered form for the professional artist — even the rare lapis lazuli which is ground to make ultramarine. There are plans to market here a new range of paints made to an eighteenth century recipe.

Shapland, High Holborn, Holborn, London

W. F. Greenwood, Stonegate, York

Top: This shop was a pawnbroker's in the late nineteenth century. The style of display remains Victorian with every inch of window space filled — even the door has a built-in show cabinet.
Bottom: This shop began in 1780 as a funeral parlour; since 1829 it has sold antiques. The crest above the door resembles the Royal Crest but actually is of Dutch origin put up for decoration. Still, the shop has Royal connections. Queen Mary often used to visit it, as commemorated in the photograph shown beside the door at the right.

Arthur Kay & Bros, Market Street, Manchester   **James Smith & Son, New Oxford Street, Bloomsbury, London**

Left: The small brass plaque under this sign says that this notice no longer applies. Right: A classic and well-loved London shop, established in 1830 and still run by the same family. Most of the staff have been in the shop for their entire working lives; one assistant used to come back to work for nothing after he had retired. Top: A master signwriter has put his distinctive stamp on the shop frontage.

Thorps, High Street, Guildford, Surrey

Thorps is everything that a bookshop ought to be, with room after room of floor-to-ceiling shelves filled with books. Customers feel there's always a chance of discovering a priceless first edition.

Andrew Block, Barter Street, Bloomsbury, London

Second Hand Shop, High Street, Wells, Norfolk

Top: Known to his friends as the doyen of the book trade, Andrew Block is an extraordinarily active nonagenarian and has been selling books since 1911. As an author, he has eight books to his credit. The disarray of his shop is illusory — every book is catalogued in long hand in his files, and he knows every title on his shelves. Bottom: It is not obvious at first sight, but someone with a sense of humour has indicated the nature of this shop's business by adding a second hand to the familiar pointed finger motif.

Fifth Avenue, Goodge St., London   **Mina Repairs, Old Kent Rd., London**

Left: One of a pair made to special order thirty years ago, but never claimed. Originally in cream and green leather (and then costing thirty pounds) this shoe was recently sprayed silver to go with the sign. Right: This sole was decorated by the present owner's predecessor at the shop, but is still proudly displayed in the window. British craftsmen generally won prizes at international exhibitions for similar pinpoint work.

Shoe Repairs, Lambs Conduit Street, Bloomsbury, London

This enamel advertisement for boot polish is kept as a decorative relic at the back of the shop.

A. E. Rice, Marylebone Lane, Marylebone, London
Mr Rice is a rarity today — a true craftsman shoe repairer. Like all such specialists, he has far
too much work to do.

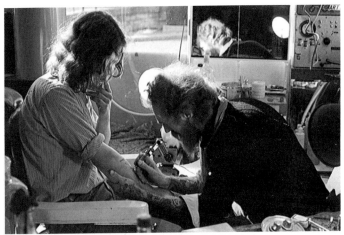

Steve, Belvedere, Bath, Avon

'Cynthia', Animal Beautician, Bacup Road, Rawtenstall, Lancashire

Top: The tattooist's work is seasonal and most in demand in summer time when the maximum area of skin is exposed. 'In the summer everyone wants aggressive designs, black panthers, eagles etc. In the autumn it's swallows and in the spring they want something soft and sentimental like roses.' Bottom: Spot the points of detail that make this poodle parlour a pedigree specimen. Lace trimmings and frills set the style for the well-bred canine customers.

Horlocks Coaches, The Hill, Northfleet, Kent

Brian Horlock makes all travel arrangements himself, and provides a very personal type of continental tour.

Funeral Director

Ernest Napier & Sons, Lancaster Road, Notting Hill, London

Known to his public as the 'undertaker' he prefers the more euphemistic title 'Funeral Director', as being more befitting the sobriety of his profession. A man of many parts, he may double as the local carpenter and joiner. Behind the scenes in his workshop he is a craftsman, proud of the finish to his made-to-measure coffins; he takes no account of the short time that his work will be seen before it is committed to the ground to rot or to the fire to burn. In his front office he is a master of tact and discretion when dealing with the bereaved. He has to organise a fairly complicated series of events at short notice, with military precison. If there is a hitch in the proceedings he is never forgotten or forgiven. When the funeral is under way he is the master of ceremonies, keeping out of the lime-light but setting the mood of the occasion by his sombre dress and quiet efficiency. He holds up the traffic with a gloved hand as the procession moves away, conducting a symphony of silence for the dead.

As one would expect, the funeral shop is sombre and discreet. Black, grey and dark shades of green and brown are used for the front, and gilded lettering is the norm. Inside, the furnishing is sparse but formal; wood panelling, a heavy desk, bentwood chairs set the required tone. The window display is a problem. There are no wares to advertise, only a service. Some firms resort to a symbolically empty window, a genteel lace curtain, or a spray of real or artificial flowers. There may be a display of monumental masonry (giving the uncomfortable impression that people have been buried just under the window), or a photograph of a cemetery or a majestic hearse. Some shops go in for images of eternity; in one shop in London there is a photograph of a calm sea, stretching uninterrupted towards the horizon; in another a tank of goldfish swimming about. There may just be a clock, a disquieting *memento mori*, or as a more brutal reminder to the passer-by, an empty coffin.

The nineteenth century was the glorious age of the funeral director, when death was celebrated with lavish ceremony. Professional mutes were employed to walk beside the hearses, which were drawn by teams of plumed horses, and the deceased were commemorated with extravagantly carved stone tombs and mausolea. But all this is changing. The modern preference is for our dead to be unseen and quickly put away without fuss. We choose our funerals to be cheap and unostentatious. For the sake of economy, firms are forced to buy in ready-made coffins of chipboard with a wood veneer. In rural districts men still stand to attention and raise their hats as the funeral procession passes. But in cities very often, as the hearse carrying the dead takes its place in the traffic queues and comes to rest at the lights, people look away, too embarrassed to acknowledge the passing of the dead. It is a sad reflection for the funeral director that after so much care his processional display is so little noticed or appreciated.

Ernest Napier & Sons, Lancaster Road, Notting Hill, London

This shop was demolished in 1976, having been under threat for five years. Brothers Howard and Barry Napier took over the business from their father, who built the front in 1904. Both interior and exterior had been perfectly preserved since that time. The Napier hearse bought in 1948 for five thousand pounds was one of only three built by Daimler on a chassis, originally designed for ambulances. Ted Darby was a bearer with Napiers from the days of horse-drawn hearses. His favourite recollection is of the time he drove a ghost. 'There were two friends who agreed to attend each other's funeral. The one who died first would come back to the other man's funeral. Well, I wasn't told about this. I drove up to the house and the undertaker opened the door. Nobody came out of the house, but he raised his hat and closed the door of the carriage as if someone was getting in. At the end of the funeral we went through the same ritual — open door, raise your hat. So I drove the empty coach back to the house. The widow opened the door and looked in. "I've done my duty, Henry" — that was all she said, and then she closed the door again and I drove off. . . . People do some strange things.'

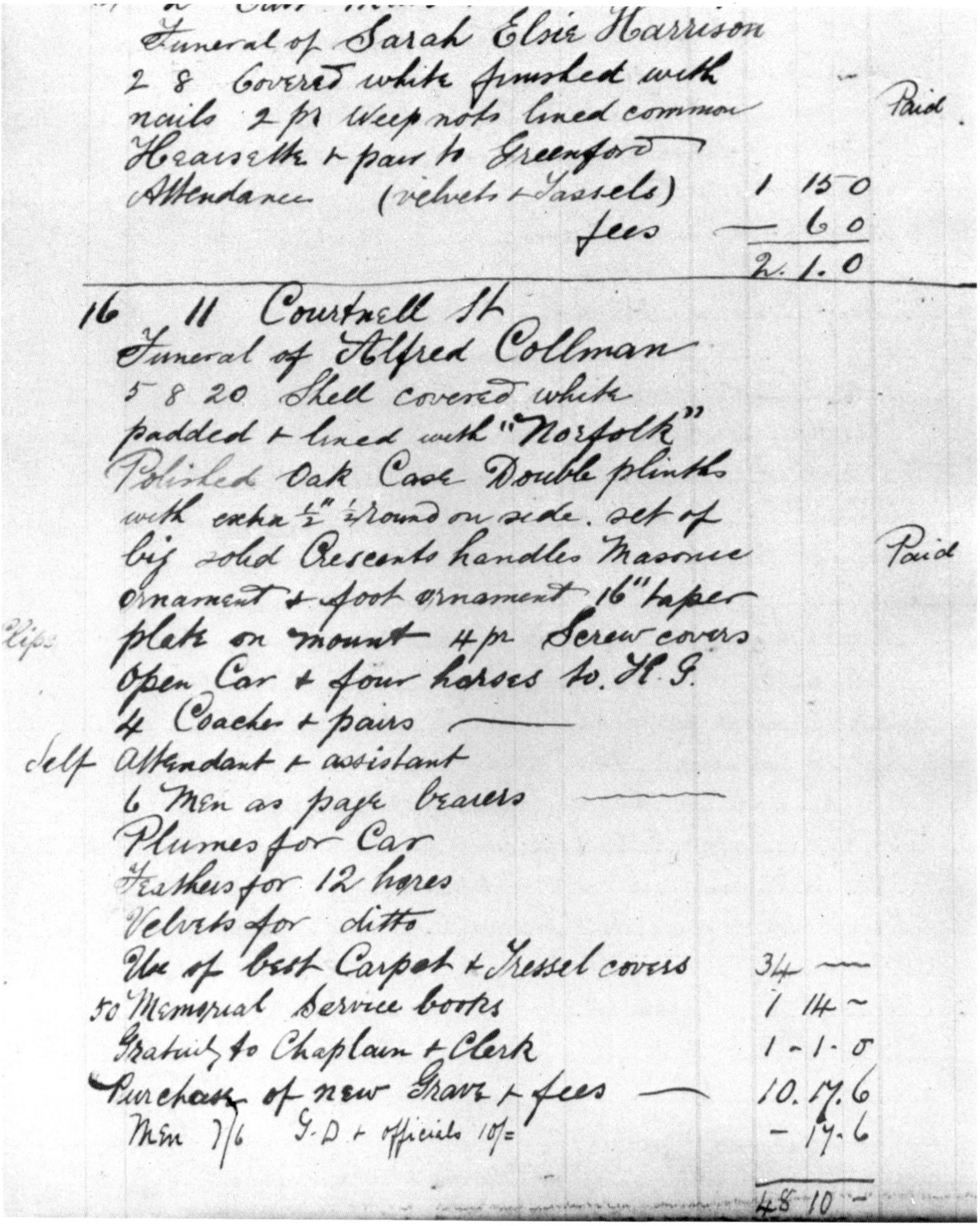

Funeral of Sarah Elsie Harrison
2 8 Covered white finished with
nails 2 pr Weep nots lined common
Hearsette & pair to Greenford
Attendance   (velvets & Tassels)   1 15 0
                    fees   — 6 0
                                              2 . 1 . 0

16   11 Courtnell St
    Funeral of Alfred Collman
5 8 20 Shell covered white
padded & lined with "Norfolk"
Polished Oak Case Double plinths
with extra ½" round on side. set of
big solid Crescents handles Masonic
ornament & foot ornament 16" taper
plate on mount 4 pr Screw covers
Open Car & four horses to. H.G.
4 Coaches & pairs ——
Self Attendant & assistant
    6 Men as page bearers   ——
    Plumes for Car
    Feathers for 12 horses
    Velvets for ditto
    Use of best Carpet & Tressel covers   34 ——
50 Memorial Service books   1 14 ~
    Gratuity to Chaplain & Clerk   1 - 1 - 0
Purchase of new Grave & fees ——   10 . 17 . 6
    Men 7/6   G.D & officials 10/=   — 17. 6
                                              48 10 —

E. M. Kendall (formerly Recknells), Dalston Lane, Dalston, London

Ernest Napier & Sons, Lancaster Road, Notting Hill, London

Left: Mourners are received in the front room at Napier's. Top right: Funeral feathermen supplied black plumes for horses, as shown (bottom right) on the Napier funeral hearse in 1912. Opposite: Napier's accounts book showing the cost of the 1912 funeral. Today even the simplest ceremony starts at one hundred pounds.

Hayes & English, Bowes Road, Wood Green, London

W. G. Miller, Essex Road, Islington, London

Top: This shop has retained all its Edwardian dignity and is well preserved considering that it faces the busy North Circular Road. Bottom: The proprietor of this shop is very proud of his trade, and despondent at the lack of interest it arouses. 'It's heartbreaking when you spend hours on a coffin and no one turns up. When I first started we used to French polish every coffin and we'd spend a whole day. Now we finish it in half an hour — it's seventy per cent cremation these days.'

Ernest Napier & Sons, Lancaster Road, Notting Hill, London
Still life with coffin — workshop interior at Napier's.

103

Hawes, Cameron Road, Seven Kings, Ilford, Essex

E. L. Wickes & Son, Denmark Hill, Camberwell, London

Hitchcock Ltd., Barking Road, Plaistow, London

Top left: A clean, simple and geometric shopfront. Even the clock contributes to the square design, which gives a feeling of repose and stability. Bottom left: At first sight it seems that the signwriter repeated himself, but there is reason behind this set of signs. When E. L. Wickes set up shop, he worked alone. When he was joined by his son he didn't want to damage the original sign, so he celebrated with a new one and announced that they were funeral furnishers — in the plural. Right: A Victorian funeral parlour door, with characteristically florid decoration.

W. F. Dolman & Son, London Road, Bath, Avon

The bust above this shop, which has overtones of the last judgement, is actually a relic of the days when the building was the Bath Eye and Ear Infirmary. The Dolman firm took over the premises in 1919.

Edmett's Signs, Lambs Conduit Street, Bloomsbury, London
The signwriter's sample box.

The Signwriter's Art

Old sign, uncovered, Liverpool

Walk up any High Street in England and witness the desecration of the art of signwriting. Until just a few years ago every shop would have its own unique and personalised sign, carved, painted or gilded by hand on wood, glass or tile. Each district would have its own writer with his distinctive style. As one London signwriter points out, 'Twenty-five years ago we could have walked all over London and on every street I could have told you who made the signs.' Not so now. Walk from Peckham to Hornsey looking for signs; more, travel from London to Newcastle, from Lower Wallop to Oswaldtwistle and everywhere you will find the same. Bleak strips of perspex in white, black and red with machine-cut letters in contrasting hues, scream out from almost every shopfront.

Here and there a perspex sign gets damaged, and behind it one may catch a glimpse of the richly seriffed tails of the golden letters of a Victorian sign. These old ones were made to last. They were bolted so firmly to the walls that modern signwriters prefer to work on top of them rather than take them down. So there remains an incalculable hoard of golden signs behind the bland façades of our High Street shops.

Happily a few fine examples remain intact and unobscured. The gilded glass signs over some of the older shopfronts have been there a hundred years and more, and they are still as crisp as the day they were made. Against the loud excesses of today's boards and posters the golden signs of yesterday seem mellow and subdued. It is odd to think that they were once considered bold, vivid, and even rather vulgar.

The joy of the signwriter's art is that no two signs were quite the same. Every one was tailor-made for the setting that it was to occupy. Untrained in the rigid discipline of Times Roman, Univers and Garamond, the signwriters had their own nameless typography, handed down from one generation to the next, with each craftsman adapting it to suit his taste. If a man was making a sign for, say, a fishmonger, he would form his letters in a way that was appropriate to the trade. He would round the serifs of the letters, perhaps, to echo the fishes' tails. A funeral director might choose the same kind of gilded glass sign as a jeweller, but the skilled signwriter would establish a contrast by making the one upright and sombre, the other flowing and decorative in style.

Travelling around the country one occasionally comes upon traces of a local tradition and style of sign work. Here and there may be found several shop signs within a small neighbourhood that share the delightful and peculiar idiosyncrasies of a man of talent. In Swindon, for instance, there are a fair number of shops with unique signs by one Charley Gaze. Charley died fourteen years ago but his memory is still fresh among the shopkeepers of the town who display his signs. He was a religious fanatic and he never failed to distribute printed tracts from the scriptures before starting work. He even signed his work, not with his own initials, but with LJC — standing for Lord Jesus Christ. Charley Gaze's work is instantly recognisable, although he would adapt his style to suit his client's trade. The shopkeeper's name was always placed centrally on the board above the shop and painted with upright lettering, artfully shaded to give a three-dimensional effect. On either side of the name he would allow his calligraphic skills full rein. In flowing copperplate script, painting freehand with a long-bristled brush, he would announce the trade carried out in the shop. He would split the inscription in two and set the separate halves on either side of the shop name, so that the words 'Grocer

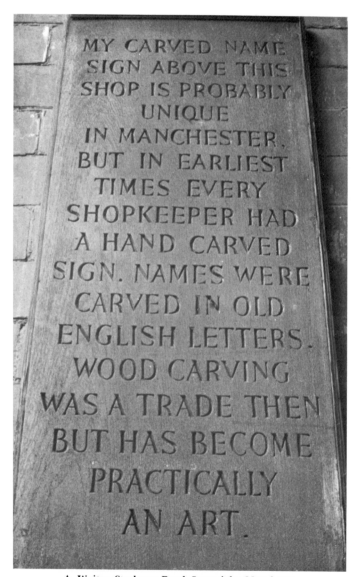

MY CARVED NAME SIGN ABOVE THIS SHOP IS PROBABLY UNIQUE IN MANCHESTER. BUT IN EARLIEST TIMES EVERY SHOPKEEPER HAD A HAND CARVED SIGN. NAMES WERE CARVED IN OLD ENGLISH LETTERS. WOOD CARVING WAS A TRADE THEN BUT HAS BECOME PRACTICALLY AN ART.

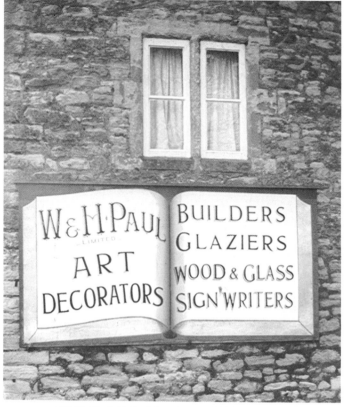

W. H. Paul, St Cuthbert Street, Wells, Somerset

A. Wojtas, Stockport Road, Longsight, Manchester

Left: Recently carved signs are extremely rare. This example from Manchester is one of two panels which tell the story of the carver's life at the side of his shop. Top right: Painted and gilded sign.

Carpenter's, Cricklade Road, Swindon, Wiltshire

Charley Gaze's *trompe-l'oeil* stone carving painting.

and Dairyman' for instance, would be counterbalanced by 'Purveyors of fine teas' on the other side. A *tour de force* by Charley Gaze is a sign outside a monumental mason's shop. Here is painted a sign as an imitation of lettering carved out of stone. Most passers-by are taken in by it.

One of the proudest sons of Bideford in North Devon was Tom Hamlyn, who won a national prize for signwriting against competition from all over England. This was back in 1904. But his signwriting shop remains there in a backstreet of the town, used as a poodle parlour now, but still gloriously emblazoned with his name in golden lettering on etched glass.

The Edmett family have been signwriters in the same workshops in Lambs Conduit Street, Bloomsbury, for five generations. Examples of the work of each generation can be seen on shops and pubs around the district. The present John Edmett's grandfather was little short of a genius. He carried away prizes for signwriting at all the international exhibitions of the day. His metier was painting and gilding in glass —the highest skill in the signwriter's repertoire. He whittled away his spare time by creating a massive inscription of the Creed, in gilded copperplate writing on a plate glass sheet eight feet high. He executed advertisements for liqueurs in the same style. He never signed his work — he said that it was meant as an advertisement for his clients and not for himself.

The sign painter works on the back of the glass, so he cannot see the effect that he is producing until he looks through from the other side. The undercoat appears as the top layer, and so there is no chance to correct mistakes. He has to get it right first time. 'Blocking' and 'blending' is the technique with which the artist paints letters with edges so that they look like three-dimensional blocks. He 'blends' the colours together to create a soft gradation where the highlights merge into the shadows.

Some lettered signs are three-dimensional behind the glass. In the earliest signs of this type the letters were carved as recesses in a plank of wood. The recesses were gilded, and the flat surface of the plank painted in a contrasting colour, often black. The glass was then laid on top. A simpler way of making this kind of sign was patented by the London firm, Brilliants. The Brilliant signs were made from stout copper sheets, and the letters embossed into the metal with steel dyes. The impressions created by the dyes were V-shaped in cross-section. The glass that was used to cover this embossed copper sheet was painted so that the whole area of copper,

apart from the letters, was masked off. Brilliants continued to make these beautiful signs until 1975 when they went out of business.

Elegant signs of letters and numbers have had a relatively brief history. Far more ancient in origin are the hanging signs that signify particular trades; the padlock or the key for the ironmonger, the hanging sheep for the tailor and so on. In the eighteenth century and before, every tradesman would signify his trade with a sign of this type. Written signs and numbers were no use because most of the population could not read or count. During the eighteenth century the old hanging signs became increasingly troublesome: 'The many pranks of wind and rain so rusted the bearings of the hinges that the musical symphonies they rendered at nights were an intolerable nuisance to the peaceful citizens'. The creaking signs not only kept the citizens awake at night, but they knocked them off their horses, and occasionally fell on top of them too. By 1762 the citizens had had enough. A law was passed that banned projecting signs beyond a certain size. Public houses retained the tradition of hanging signs, but most shops changed over to the flat sign, fixed flush to the wall of the building. The traditional hanging shop sign is becoming increasingly rare.

High Street, Tenterden, Kent

Fish in gilded wood — an appropriate indication of this shop's trade, complete with hook, line and rod.

J. Blundell & Son, Wardour Street, Soho, London

James Smith & Son, New Oxford Street, London

Miles & Son, High Street, Dorchester, Dorset

Smiths Snuff Shop, Charing Cross Road, London

T. L. Hamlyn & Son, Bideford, Devon

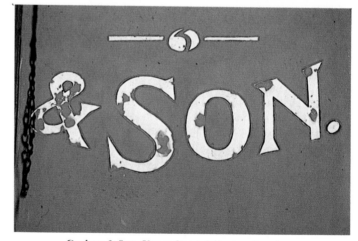

Cooksey & Son, Upper Street, Islington, London

Delnero & Sons, Corn Street, Witney, Oxfordshire

A. Brown & Sons, Moorgate, City of London

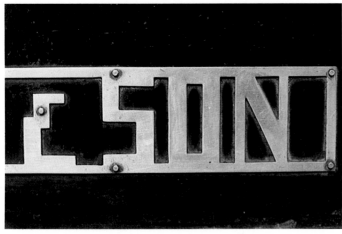

Bland & Son, Notting Hill Gate, London

James Smith & Son, New Oxford Street, London

White & Son, Fore Street, Topsham, Devon

M. Harris & Sons, New Oxford Street, London

J. W. Rainbird, Romford Road, Manor Park, London

Bert's, East Street, Old Kent Road, London

Coombs, Gloucester Road, Kensington, London

Goss, Old Market Street, Bristol

Evans, Warren Street, Fitzrovia, London

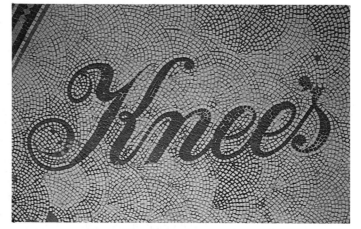

Knees, Albert Street, Penzance, Cornwall

Above and preceding pages: Details of signs which show the continuity of families in shopkeeping, as well as the varieties of signwriting style.

Watson's, Collingwood Street, Newcastle

Jackson's, Norton Road, Stockton-on-Tees

W. S. Wright, New Bank, Halifax, West Yorkshire

Holgate Road Fisheries, Holgate Road, York

The front door of a shop is like the expression on a human face; it reveals much of the character within.

Hawken & Sons (Tailor), Truro, Cornwall

G. Gray (Chemist), Berwick-upon-Tweed

Salmon's (Ironmonger), Westham Lane, London

The Victoria Bakery, High Street, Barnet, Herts.

A. Saunders Southampton Row, London

Pen-y-Darran (Model Shop), Trim Bridge, Bath,

Hanging signs are rather uncommon now, though there was a time when every shop would have one. Before the late eighteenth century the population was largely illiterate, and so shops and taverns were marked by hanging symbols. These became a hazard to horsemen and pedestrians, and in 1797 a statute was passed, forbidding projecting signs. Inn signs seem to have by-passed this law rather more successfully than shop signs.

Hayes, Saddler, Market Place, Cirencester, Gloucestershire

Gable End Mural, Moor Court, Hendon, Sunderland, Durham

Above: This is not a shop, but a painting of one. The only thing that is real is the Moor Court sign on the right. The painting, done by local Jarrow artist Ken Watts, developed out of a community arts project in Sunderland's East End and is taken from an old photograph of a ship's chandlers that used to be in this dockland area. The mural has become a local landmark since its completion in 1975.

Architecture

To the pedestrian in a shopping thoroughfare the line of projecting shopfronts provides the dominant architectural experience of the street. Yet architects have largely chosen to neglect this area of their profession, for shop design is considered to belong on the borderline of the field of architecture.

The distinguished Victorian architect F. P. Cockerell, credited in *The Builder* with the design of a fine shopfront in Bond Street, sharply repudiated it with the retort that he hoped that the next time he was honoured by a mention in *The Builder* it would be for something of more interest to its readers than a shopfront. But two of his contemporaries were apologetically enthusiastic about shopfront design. Victor Delasseux and John Elliott produced a series of projected designs for shopfronts in 1855 and in their introduction wrote:

It may not at first sight appear a very dignified employment for heads of the profession to use their talents in designing shopfronts and street façades, but in reality few classes of subject afford such scope for inventive genius and none where its efforts would be more appreciated, or exercise so favourable an influence on the taste of the multitude.

The heads of the profession seem to have been unmoved, for although Delasseux's and Elliott's generation produced some distinguished shopfronts, the names of the architects involved went unrecorded. And to this day the standard reference books on architecture make only passing reference to shopfronts.

There are several reasons for the profession's disenchantment with shop architecture. For a start there is no area of architecture that is so dominated by fashion. The architect likes to build for posterity; the shopkeeper wants to keep his

Cridlan & Walker, Great Malvern, Worcs.
A Regency Gothic shop — a rarity today.

public face constantly up-to-date. This conflict applies as much today as it did in 1841 when the *Westminster Review* commented that an architect could hardly be expected to put much heart into his work when it was likely to be ruthlessly mutilated as soon as it was carried out, if not before, just to please the 'demon of fashion'. Indeed some of the nineteenth-century shops of Regent Street were built with their structural support on the inside, with the deliberate intention that the fronts could be very easily altered.

Another of the shopkeeper's priorities strikes at the very heart of architectural principle. The shopkeeper tends to want the greatest possible window area in which to display his goods; the ideal window as far as he is concerned is a massive expanse of glass with the minimum visible means of support. This idea is anathema to the architect. It is a basic and logical tenet of architecture that a building should be heaviest at the base, becoming progressively lighter towards the top. The architect likes to give a sense of security to the user of a building by giving some evidence that the building is held up by a reliable system of support. A building that consists effectively of a gaping hole beneath a solid façade seems both visually unbalanced and structurally insecure. Successive generations of architects have been conscious of this problem, but none can be said to have solved it. The problem may be closest to solution in some examples of modern architecture in which the whole façade consists of a wall of glass. Whatever its other faults, a building of this kind with a shop at street level does not look top-heavy.

A related problem for the shop architect is to build a shopfront in keeping with the building in which it is contained. This can be achieved when the whole façade, including the

Ironmonger & Brazier

A superb example of fine Victorian street architecture, this building was proposed in 1856 by Victor Delassaux and John Elliott. Their concern was to design the shopfront to reflect exactly the trade which would be practised within: 'A little extra expense in the façade will not be thrown away in this business, the front affording the best opportunity of showing what the proprietor can effect with the material in which he deals.' The architects went on to suggest an oak balcony, bronzed wrought iron work with burnished or gilt mouldings and deep blue panelling.

Tanners, Wyle Cop, Shrewsbury, Shropshire

A. H. Hale, Argyle Street, Bath, Avon

Tallow (kitchen) Chandler, Couching Street, Watlington, Oxfordshire

Top left: This building is a perfect example of eighteenth century shop architecture. Though the only means of identification here is a brass plaque on the door, there might once have been a hanging sign to announce the family's wine trade. Bottom left: A perfectly preserved shopfront of 1833, with its original sign intact upon the brickwork. A tallow chandler was a dealer in candles made from fat, as opposed to wax. Right: A. H. Hale was one of the first to have a shopfront with plate glass. This shop was founded in 1826 and the present front erected two years later.

shopfront, is designed as a whole. But very often the shopfront has to be superimposed on a building of an earlier period and it is difficult to achieve harmony. The Victorian architects failed in this respect as much as our own. A Victorian shopfront with pillars in the classical style looks out of place when built on to a mediaeval façade. Likewise a modern plate glass front will never look right on a Georgian building. However, we are so accustomed to divorcing shop architecture from that of the surrounding streets that we fail to notice these juxtapositions. And for some people it is the hotchpotch of architecture of different periods that gives such charm to our towns.

The history of shop design is closely tied up with the social history of trading, and the development of building methods is as much involved as design. In mediaeval times most trade was carried out at street markets and with itinerant pedlars who came to the door. The 'bulk shop' of this time was only a slightly sophisticated version of the street-market stall. It consisted of a board that acted as a shutter over a window. The board was hinged at the bottom and swung down on to a set of legs to make a table. An overhanging roof, called the pent roof, projected over the table and the footpath as well, and provided shelter for the destitute at night.

Another form of early shop, and one which still exists today, was nothing more than the front room of a private house. For the craftsman shopkeeper of all periods, the domestic dwelling served as workshop, sales outlet and home. The shopkeeper of the Middle Ages would open the shutters before breakfast, close them again before he went to bed, and the shop would remain open all the time in between. Shutters are an archetypal feature of shops and date back, probably, to the very earliest shop premises. Nearly all shops had shutters until around 1870, when there was a growing tendency to leave shop windows uncovered at night, with lights inside to deter burglars. Jewellers and other shops with valuable stock have shutters still, and so do many fishmongers and greengrocers. These latter shops are, architecturally, a primitive type. Being open to the street, without windows, they are little more than covered market stalls. There is evidence for the antiquity of shutters in the word itself. Why in speech do we say that a shop is 'shut' when the written notice on the door always says 'closed'? A convincing explanation is that the Anglo-Saxon word 'shut' is a spoken relic from the days when most people were illiterate, and the word 'closed' was only used in this sense when the absence of shutters made it unclear whether the shop was open or not.

The eighteenth century saw a boom in domestic architecture and it was at this time that many purpose-built shops were incorporated into the new façades. The shopfronts of

Post Office, Stiffkey, Norfolk

A. J. Faith, East Street, Chichester, Sussex

Shutters used to be the only indication of whether or not a shop was open for business. In the late nineteenth century, many shopkeepers began to leave their windows uncovered

this period are in harmony with the streets that contain them because they were designed together as a unity. Their simplicity of design is partly a result of technical necessity. Windows had to be small because only small panes of glass could be made at the time. 'Crown bullion' glass was made by blowing a bubble of glass, then spinning it so that it flattened. This type of glass can be recognised by the central knob which is left by the glassblower's iron. Another type of early glass was blown into a mould and is called 'Norman slab' since it was introduced into this country during the eleventh century. The small panes of glass were mounted in an elegant wooden framework. This lattice-like structure of the Georgian shop window is a strong architectural feature that gives the impression of an enclosure rather than a cavity. So it gives a weightier base to a building than later shop windows, glazed with larger panes and criss-crossed with fewer sash bars.

With the coming of the nineteenth century the increasingly decorative style of Regency architecture is reflected in the shopfronts of the period. Decorative tracery appears over the doors and in the arches of the windows. The windows themselves are often bowed. The fashion for ornamental ironwork is sometimes demonstrated by lace-like fringes of painted iron above the shop fascia. Classical orders were all the rage, and many a Regency shop features Ionic columns,

beautifully carved in wood, supporting the façade. The Regency Gothic style, which made country homes look like castles, is rare in shop design, but there is one surviving example, a butcher's shop, in Malvern.

Possibly the most revolutionary influence on shop design was the introduction of plate glass in 1827. Like many similar revolutions it took some time for its presence to be felt. One of the earliest shopfronts designed to incorporate the new plate glass was built in 1828 for a chemist's shop in Argyle Street, Bath. Here the individual pieces of glass are still fairly small, but the window as a whole is taller and more spacious than any that had come before. Between 1830 and 1860 the size of the glass used in shop windows increased gradually. There was a tendency for the windows to be designed in upright strips, the panes of glass averaging about seven feet high by three feet wide, adjacent panes being separated by narrow pillars of wood, which often curved together at the top to form an arch. This gave a strong vertical emphasis to the window in contrast to the horizontal emphasis of the Georgian style, with its criss-cross framework. By 1860 panes of glass eight feet by fourteen feet could be made and windows of this size were used at that time in the shopfront of Asprey's of Bond Street, London.

Decorative detail is a characteristic of much Victorian architecture, and Victorian shopfronts were as ornate as any

T. Atkinson, Market Place, Darlington, Durham

Tessiers, Bond Street, Mayfair, London

after business hours, with lights inside. Today, a few tradesmen, jewellers amongst them, still literally shut up their shops at night.

Slaters Luncheon Rooms, Piccadilly, London

Gurd's Outfitters, Station Road, Taunton, Somerset

Three examples of Victorian shopfronts. Variations of the classical columns of which the Victorians were so fond are found on all three fronts. For Henry Taylor (left) they served a strong functional purpose; at Slaters Luncheon Rooms (top) they provided a grand and imposing façade; while at Gurd's Outfitters (bottom), they are so well incorporated into the design of the shop as to go almost unnoticed. An unusual feature of Gurd's frontage is the decorative tiles either side of the shop.

Henry Taylor, Commercial Street, Bournemouth

J. E. Evans, Warren Street, Fitzrovia, London

A good shopfront in which the ceramic tiles, the glass sign and the artificially
grained door harmonise together.

other buildings of the period, if not more so. In the eyes of
some critics this embellishment was gratuitous and over-
done. Henry Russell Hitchcock has written (1954), 'Slapdash handling of conventional Greek and Roman decorative
elements gave way to an equally slapdash imitation of Italian
Renaissance'. The constant re-hashing of classical architectural themes even came in for some criticism at the time.
The *Westminster Review* (Oct 1841) records that 'thousands
of diminutive copies of the same originals are to be seen all
over the town, all apparently turned out of the same manu-
factory . . . for which reason we wonder that no one should
have established one where the columns may be purchased
ready for use like chimney pots. This would save a great deal
of trouble in making designs . . . it simply being sufficient to
write so many columns, Athenian etc., size so and so, and so
many feet of plate glass between them'. *The Builder* was
another journal that objected to the classical style, on the
grounds that the openings that were left between the
columns for windows were too large for classical proportion:
'why should a style be employed merely for the purpose of
being mangled?'

The Classical and Renaissance styles were not the only
ones the Victorians borrowed for the purposes of shop architecture. In 1838 we hear of a shop in the 'Louis XIV style'. In
1841 a shop described as 'neo-Elizabethan' was put up in

Campkin & Blackstone, Market Street, Cambridge

This Art Nouveau shopfront was hidden for years behind a plywood façade and found when the façade was stripped to make a new front. The windows with their curving tracery are original but the door is a later addition. In 1923 (left) the shop was featured in the *Cambridge Chronicle*.

Oxford Street, and in 1843 appeared the most spectacular of all, described at the time as 'one of the most remarkable of the London palaces of trade' — a shop modelled upon the glorious Moorish style of the Alhambra. Sadly none of these strange-sounding hybrids remain.

The increasing extravagance of Victorian shop architecture and design could only be carried out through a parallel expansion of craft skills and techniques. The buildings of the Great Exhibition of 1851 in Hyde Park (which later became the Crystal Palace at Sydenham) showed what could be achieved with iron and glass. Inside these great glass pavilions were displayed the accomplishments of British craftsmen. The craft trades were at a high peak, and the finest Victorian shopfronts and interiors are as much a credit to the builders who constructed and enriched them, the cabinet makers who fitted them out with mahogany and embellished them with carvings, the signpainters who created glorious extravaganzas of gilded glass, as to the architects who conceived them.

Towards the end of the century art and architecture throughout Europe took a turn, some would say towards decadence. The new art was called Art Nouveau, signifying its European origin. The flowing arabesques, the fertile and distorted shapes of Art Nouveau made their appearance in

W. H. Smith & Sons, Embarkation Lounge, Southampton Dock, Hampshire

Dietz, High Street, Gateshead, Durham

Left: Another 1930s trend was for buildings — and housing in particular — to reflect the ship architecture of the period. This embarkation lounge and book shop are good examples. Right: The angular letters match the design of this 1930s butcher's frontage.

English architecture, including shopfronts, but only as a watered-down version of the Continental style. Far more extravagant examples of Art Nouveau shopfronts can be seen in Paris and Brussels. In England Art Nouveau made its influence felt in pottery, glass design and lettering. The style is reflected in many shop signs of the period, and in one great achievement of applied art: the pictorial ceramic tiles by W. J. Neatby in the meat hall at Harrods.

The 1930s heralded another distinct period of architecture which contributed some distinguished shop designs. The predominant style was probably the last of the 'total' styles in the history of art. It reached furniture, ceramics, cinema design, and graphics as well as architecture and painting, and has been labelled 'Art Deco'. This style is characterised by geometric structures made up of squares, circles, rectangles and semicircles with details streamlined and simplified in the extreme. The period between the wars saw a rapid development of machines and new materials. The shop fittings were factory-made and mass-produced to uniform patterns. Those whose business was fashion were eager to shed the Edwardian cloak from their shops and go modern. The shopkeepers who could not afford a chrome façade and neon lights made the best of another pot of paint. The new machine-made shop, with its hard lines and geo-

metric shapes, provided a startling contrast to the 'hand-made' façades and interiors of the shops built at the turn of the century. Yet the craft skills were still in evidence, channelled now through industry, and creating a personal touch and a note of humour within a framework of good clean functional design.

Since the war the architecture of our shops has been dominated by a social revolution in the shopping habit. The small old shops at the heart of our cities have been torn down to make way for the ever-larger new stores and the car parks that seem to be a necessary extension of them. Once again, technical advances have had an influence over design. Steel girders and ferro-concrete have meant that vast spaces can be spanned without supporting pillars. The modern store is like a vast auditorium, and the architect has affinities with the theatre director. He studies the lighting effects, the flow patterns of the people, the most seductive arrangement of the props and even the background music. Everything is put on show with the maximum impact. But for the shopper who shrinks from the bright lights of the supermarket, there remain here and there those more modest shops that we have celebrated. In these small establishments individuals are pampered and eccentrics are understood. Here the nation of shopkeepers is very much at home — business as usual.

Modiste, St Andrews Street, Cambridge

J. Leslie Ltd., New Bridgate, Leeds, Yorkshire

In clothes shops as in almost everything else in the 1930s, the fashion in design was for streamlined, geometric graphics, whether on the frontage above the shop or on doors, windows and the floors of entryways. Notice, too, that both these shops were designed with highly recessed doors, to give maximum space for window display. The frosted glass over Modiste's both provides plenty of light in the workshop and enhances the frontage.

Bibliography

Adburgham, Alison. *Shops and Shopping 1800–1914* (George Allen and Unwin, London, 1964)

Artley, Alexandra. *The Golden Age of Shop Design: European Shop Interiors* (Architectural Press, London, 1975)

Cohn, Nik. *Today There Are No Gentlemen* (Weidenfeld and Nicholson, London, 1971)

Dan, Horace and Willmott, Morgan. *English Shop-fronts Old and New* (Batsford, London, 1907)

Davis, Dorothy. *History of Shopping* (Routledge and Kegan Paul, London, 1966)

Delassaux, Victor and Elliot, John. *Architecture of Shop-fronts* (John Weale, London, 1855)

Edwards, Arthur T. *The Architecture of Shops* (Chapman and Hall, London, 1933)

Eldridge, Mary. 'The Plate Glass Shop-front' *Architectural Review* (London, March 1958)

Heal, Ambrose. *London Tradesman Cards of the XVIIIth Century* (Batsford, London, 1925)

Hillier, Bevis. *Art Deco* (Studio Vista, London, 1968)

J. S. 100. The Story of Sainsbury's (J. Sainsbury, 1969)

Jeffreys, James B. *Retail Trading In Britain 1850–1950* (Cambridge University Press, Cambridge, 1954)

Lambton, Lucinda. *Vanishing Victoriana* (Phaidon, Oxford, 1976)

Levy, Herman. *The Shops of Britain* (Kegan Paul, London, 1948)

Opie, Robert. *The Pack Age Exhibition Catalogue* (Victoria and Albert Museum, London, 1976)

Phelp, R. K. *The Shopkeeper's Guide* (Houlston and Stoneman, London, 1853)

Rothwell, Tom S. *A Nation of Shopkeepers* (Herbert Joseph, London, 1947)

Szasz, Kathleen. *Petishism, Pet Cults of the Western World* (Hutchinson, London, 1968)

Taylor, Herbert. 'Shops' *Architectural Review* (London, Feb. 1957)

Waugh, Norah. *Corsets and Crinolines* (Batsford, London, 1954)

Westwood, B. & N. *Smaller Retail Shops* (Architectural Press, London, 1937)